David Gants
dgants@unb.ca
Electronic Text Centre
Department of English
University of New Brunswick

OTHER TITLES IN THE CODENOTES SERIES

CodeNotes for J2EE: EJB, JDBC, JSP, and Servlets

CodeNotes for .NET

CodeNotes for Java: Intermediate and Advanced Language Features

CodeNotes for VB.NET

CodeNotes for Web-Based UI

CodeNotes® for XML

Edited by GREGORY BRILL

CodeNotes® for XML

NEW YORK

Published in the United States by Random House, Inc., New York, and simultaneously in Canada by Random House of Canada Limited, Toronto.

Grateful acknowledgment is made to Netscape Communications Corporation for permission to reprint Netscape Browser Window. Copyright © 2002 by Netscape Browser Corporation. Used with permission.

Library of Congress cataloging-in-publication data is available.

ISBN 0-8129-9191-5

Website address: www.atrandom.com

Printed in the United States of America on acid-free paper

2 4 6 8 9 7 5 3

First Edition

Using CodeNotes

PHILOSOPHY

The CodeNotes philosophy is that the core concepts of any technology can be presented succinctly. Building from many years of consulting and training experience, the CodeNotes series is designed to make you productive in a technology in as short a time as possible.

CODENOTES POINTERS

Throughout the book, you will encounter CodeNotes Pointers, such as CN XM000000. These pointers are links to additional content available online at the CodeNotes website. To use a pointer, simply go to http://www.codenotes.com and type the pointer number in the provided entry field. The website will direct you to an article or example that provides additional information about the topic.

Should any direct web links in this CodeNote change or become inactive, the CodeNotes website will provide updated links. You can access these updated links via CodeNotes pointer CN XM000101.

WHAT YOU NEED TO KNOW BEFORE CONTINUING

This book is written for software developers interested in learning XML and related tools such as XSLT, SAX, DOM, CSS, XPath/XLink, and Schemas. XML is simple enough to understand and use that any experience working with a structured programming language or environment such as Java, C++, Visual Basic, Perl, or even basic familiarity with HTML is all that is required to learn and master XML.

Although many tools exist to help the developer work with XML, knowledge of these tools is not a requirement to understand or work with the examples in this CodeNote. You can obtain surprisingly sophisticated results in a very short time using a simple text editor and a web browser.

If you are interested in developing software that leverages XML, later chapters of this CodeNote provide tutorials and examples based on two commonly used languages: Java and Visual Basic. Note that programming experience, while helpful, is not a prerequisite; Chapters 1 through 5 provide a complete overview of XML and related technologies and do not involve programming.

About the Authors

BRENT WILLIAMS is director of training for Infusion Development Corporation. Brent has worked in a variety of product development, training, and consulting positions for corporations in New York, Tokyo, and various cities in Canada. Brent spends his free time canoeing, mountain biking, backpacking, and otherwise enjoying the great outdoors. Brent lives in a farmhouse in Chatham, New Jersey.

CRAIG WILLS is a writer and researcher for Infusion Development Corporation. He has worked in technical documentation at a variety of institutions in both Canada and the United States, including major banks, Internet consulting firms, and software component developers. In his spare time, Craig enjoys competitive swimming, listening to punk and ska music, and writing fiction. Craig currently lives in Niagara-on-the-Lake, Ontario.

MICHAEL VAN ATTER is a software consultant with Infusion Development Corporation. He specializes in web development, and has worked on some of the most popular Canadian news websites and e-commerce sites. Michael has also consulted for large financial institutions. He was born in Canada and still lives in Oakville, Ontario, where he enjoys racing his car at Mosport International Raceway and playing hockey and football.

More information about the authors and Infusion Development Corporation can be found at www.infusiondev.com/codenotes.

Acknowledgments

First, thanks to John Gomez, who saw the potential of the CodeNotes idea before anyone else, and who introduced me to Random House. Without John, there would be no CodeNotes. John, you are a true friend, a real visionary. I'd also like to thank Annik LaFarge, who fearlessly championed the series and whose creativity, enthusiasm, and publishing savvy has been instrumental in its creation. Thank you to Mary Bahr, our unflappable editor, who paved the way and crafted the marketing. Thank you to Ann Godoff, whose strength, decisiveness, and wisdom gave CodeNotes just the momentum it needed. And, of course, the production, sales, and business teams at Random House, with particular thanks to Howard Weill, Jean Cody, and Richard Elman.

On the Infusion Development side, thank you to Pete Chiu for his contribution to the chapter on Schemas. Thank you to the CodeNotes reviewers, who gave us invaluable feedback and suggestions on our early drafts. And thank you to the entire cast and crew of Infusion Development Corporation, who have supported and encouraged this venture throughout. I know CodeNotes was extremely trying, tough to do, and involved an awesome amount of research, writing, and editing, but here it is . . . as we envisioned it.

—Gregory Brill

Contents

CodeNotes® for XML

Chapter 1

—

INTRODUCTION

ORIENTATION

What Is XML?

Extensible Markup Language (XML) is a globally accepted, vendor-independent standard for representing structured, text-based data. An XML document is a perfect medium in which to encapsulate any kind of information that can be arranged or structured in some way. For example, an XML document can contain a list of personal or business contacts, books in a library's card catalogue, or products in a warehouse.

If we looked at any one of these examples—say, the library card catalogue—in the more traditional "table-oriented" view with which most developers would be familiar, we would see something like the following:

book_isbn	book_genre	Firstname	middlename	Lastname	title
0812589041	Science Fiction	Orson	Scott	Card	Ender's Game
0883853280	biography	William		Dunham	Euler: The Master of Us All

Table 1.1 A card catalog in a flat table format

An XML document, on the other hand, would present this information hierarchically, where the column names would become tags or possibly "attributes." For example:

```
<?xml version="1.0"?>
<books>
  <book>
    <isbn>0812589041</isbn>
    <genre>science fiction</genre>
    <author>
      <firstname>Orson</firstname>
      <middlename>Scott</middlename>
      <lastname>Card</lastname>
    </author>
    <title>Enders Game</title>
    <year>1985</year>
  </book>
  <book>
    <isbn>0883853280</isbn>
    <genre>biography</genre>
    <author>
      <firstname>William</firstname>
      <middlename/>
      <lastname>Dunham</lastname>
    </author>
    <title>Euler The Master of Us All</title>
    <year>1999</year>
  </book>
</books>
```

Listing 1.1 The card catalog as XML

Listing 1.1 is included to give you a first look at XML, which can be overwhelming compared to a familiar table structure. However, as you become more familiar with XML, you will see that this structure has many important advantages over a traditional table.

XML and HTML

It can help to think of XML at its most basic level as being very similar to a HyperText Markup Language (HTML) web page. However, the tags in an XML document do not have a fixed meaning the way they do in HTML (e.g., <bold>, <body>, etc.) When a developer writes an XML document, he or she decides on the names of the elements (e.g., book, title, year, and author) and the data the elements will contain (e.g., the <year> tags contain the year the book was published). The developer chooses his elements with the expectation that some client application exists that will read the XML file and be written to process those particular elements in some way. Referring back to Listing 1.1, one can imagine that there is a book-search software application running on a computer in the library that reads XML files with this structure (perhaps receiving them via the Web from some central server), allowing library patrons to search for the books they wish to check out.

What Is XML Used For?

One misconception regarding XML is that it is simply an alternate way of transporting and storing data. However, that is only one small facet of how XML is used today. To give only a few examples, XML can be used to:

- invoke methods on a remote server through a firewall (this protocol is called SOAP)
- represent relational database data such that it can be easily translated into HTML, viewable by any browser without programming
- store configuration and deployment data for applications, providing operating-system-independent formats for initialization/configuration files
- create template documents describing the various fields and attributes of a business form

XML Tools and Technologies

In spite of its power and wide range of uses, XML itself is very straightforward. The more subtle aspects of XML do not have to do with XML itself, but rather with various third-party applications and technologies such as XML editors and authoring tools, and XML-related APIs.

XML Authoring Tools

XML files can become very large and may have many layers of nested elements. While the basic grammar of XML is relatively simple, finding a deeply buried element in a large document, or resolving a missed "/" or mismatched tag will very quickly try the patience of most software developers. Therefore, many tools have been developed to address this need. One can, of course, work with any simple text editor, but you can find a listing of some popular XML authoring tools in Chapter 3.

Translation and Styling

In addition to applications that make writing XML documents easier, there are a number of technologies that can actually extend XML's capabilities. Most web browsers are capable of displaying XML files. Internet Explorer, for example, will show an XML file as a dynamic collapsible tree much like a simple Windows File Explorer; you can click on nodes to open them and reveal their child elements, or close them to get to a top-level view of the XML document. Suppose, however, you would like your XML document to display just like a web page with proper formatting and, perhaps, a colored background? There are two ways to do this:

1. Cascading Style Sheets (CSS): CSS files are text files containing format information. CSS is an older technology developed for HTML and uses a specialized scripting language.
2. Extensible Stylesheet Language Transformations (XSLT): Where CSS files are written in a specialized script language, XSLT documents are actually written in XML. An XSLT file maps XML elements into HTML tags and, in so doing, an XSLT file is used to actually translate an XML file into an HTML file.

The separation of data and presentation using either technology allows for a much cleaner and more efficient application design.

Querying

While the XML specification defines a structure for encapsulating data, it does not have any prescribed method for querying the data in an XML document. A technology known as XPath, however, does provide a mechanism for querying an XML file. If you are familiar with relational databases, you can think of XPath as XML's much less sophisticated brand of SQL (Structured Query Language). By way of example, the XPath expression `[/stocks/stock[1.0 > @price/text()]]` will return all penny stocks from an appropriately structured XML file.

Programming with XML

In order to read an XML document, an application must parse it. The process of parsing is complex; a parser must take a text document, cut it up into meaningful segments (while making certain that these segments are correctly formed and that they conform to the rules of the language), and store the data and elements in memory. Writing a proper parser for any language or grammar is no easy task, and XML would not have caught on as a standard unless there also existed a freely available parser with a friendly programming interface to relieve the developer of this task. Fortunately, there are two: The Simple API for XML (SAX) and the Document Object Model (DOM). Ultimately, a developer can use either API to read an XML file and extract data from it. The approach taken by each of these two APIs, however, is different, as follows:

- DOM is a *passive* API. DOM reads an entire XML document, creates a tree structure in memory, and gives the developer read and write access to this tree. DOM must process the entire file and bring it into memory before a developer may access it.
- SAX is an *active* API. SAX will actually call methods on your application (or fire events) as it moves through the XML document. You can think of SAX as adhering to an event-driven model, triggering events in your application whenever it encounters anything important your application needs to know about, such as an element, text data, etc. Note that SAX does not allow modification of the XML document.

DOM and SAX are two different APIs useful for parsing, reading, and (to a small extent in the case of DOM) manipulating XML. Each API has strengths and weaknesses that will be explained in Chapters 6 and 7.

Integrating XML with Your World

XML's popularity is due to the sheer usefulness of the technology. By defining a standard, vendor-independent format that can represent any kind of data, the uses for XML are boundless. Database vendors have taken notice of XML and are making their systems XML-friendly.

You may recall from the earlier section in this chapter, "Translation and Styling," that an XML file can easily be translated to HTML via XSLT. The simplicity of this translation technology makes XML an ideal way to return data from a database since it can so easily be translated into a web-based report. CSS or additional XSLT can then be used to further enhance the appearance of the HTML page. As we will see, database vendors are quick to take advantage of these capabilities.

Upcoming XML Technologies

The XML family of technologies represents a tremendously fast-moving field where products, capabilities, and interoperability change daily. New standards are on the way for areas such as vector graphics (SVG), distributed computing (SOAP), and changes to HTML (XHTML). In addition, many industries have embraced XML as a standard for communicating specific types of information. For example, the financial industry is slowly accepting FIXML as a standard for transmitting financial information between institutions. In the next few years, you should expect to see many more standards that are based directly on XML.

ROAD MAP

This CodeNote is divided into 8 chapters. The first three chapters provide the essential background information for using XML, and the remaining chapters show specific methods, tools, and extensions that make XML such a useful and powerful tool for describing data.

1. Introduction: This chapter (which you are currently reading) contains an overview of XML and the XML technologies and a short history of XML.
2. Installation: This chapter describes the installation of several of the common XML tools. If you are already working in an XML-ready environment, you can skip this chapter.
3. XML Essentials: The XML Essentials chapter will introduce you to the fundamental grammar of XML and you will learn about elements, character text, and attributes. In addition, Chapter 3 covers the concept of a Document Type Definition (DTD), which can be used to define the specific syntax or structure of an XML document.
4. Styling with CSS: Although CSS is a technology most often used for HTML pages, it can also be applied to XML. Many companies have leveraged their existing CSS definitions to new applications that are based on XML data. In Chapter 4, you will learn the basics of CSS as applied to XML.
5. XSLT and XPath: XSLT and XPath are among the most important extensions to XML. This chapter will show you how to translate an XML document into another form (whether XML, HTML, or raw text), and how to search through the document for specific nodes using the XPath query language.
6. Programming with DOM: The first of the XML APIs (DOM) provides a tree-based model of an XML document. DOM is incredibly useful for manipulating XML inside code. This chapter will illustrate the major features of the DOM API, and will provide examples in both Java and Visual Basic.
7. Programming with SAX: Because of its simplicity, the SAX API can be used in places where DOM requires too much overhead in terms of memory and processing. This chapter will illustrate SAX using examples in both Java and Visual Basic.

8. XML Schemas: Chapter 3 introduced the Document Type Definition (DTD) standard. The DTD was a critical component in the early days of XML. However, the more recent XML Schema standard replaces the basic DTD and provides a much richer set of features for validating an XML document. This chapter illustrates the power of the XML Schema standard.

ADDITIONAL MATERIAL

The CodeNotes website (http://www.codenotes.com) contains supplementary material not included in the text of this CodeNote. In addition to the articles referenced by various CodeNotes Pointers throughout this book, the website gives you access to several major articles on topics that are important, but considered outside the scope of the book itself. These include the following:

1. XML and Relational Databases CN XM000102—This article is a tutorial on how to implement XML as a medium technology when using one of three major relational databases: Microsoft SQL Server 2000, Oracle 8i, and IBM DB2. Topics covered include inserting XML documents into a database, extracting information from a database in XML format, and implementing your own XML/database solution for when the database you are using is not overtly XML-compliant.
2. W3C Grammars CN XM000103—The World Wide Web Consortium has produced recommendations for a variety of XML grammars. XML grammars are set vocabularies of XML elements and attributes used for a specific purpose, or in a specific field. Grammars covered in this article include SVG (an XML grammar for displaying vector graphics over the web); XHTML (an XML recreation of HTML); and Simple Object Access Protocol (SOAP), an XML grammar that enables remote access in distributed programming environments.
3. XLink and XPointer CN XM000104—This article will cover two W3C draft standards that provide powerful intra- and inter-XML document linking, comparable (but vastly superior to) hyperlinks in HTML.
4. Sample XML Architectures CN XM000105—This article presents a series of typical business scenarios. It then compares solutions to the problems using traditional technologies and XML. These case studies are intended to demonstrate clearly

where XML can be used in the business world, as well as its potential benefits and drawbacks.

5. XML Programming with Perl CN XM000106 and XML Programming with JavaScript CN XM000107—The code samples throughout this book are presented either in Java, Visual Basic, or both. These two articles provide brief coverage of how to leverage XML using two other popular programming languages: Perl and JavaScript.

ABOUT THE VENDOR

World Wide Web Consortium

XML, CSS, and almost all the other technologies discussed in this CodeNote are first and foremost *specifications* published by the World Wide Web Consortium (W3C, http://www.w3.org). The W3C is an open standards body; that is, a kind of committee where different representatives of the development community collaboratively decide on standards for the Web. The W3C was founded by Tim Berners-Lee, who is considered by many to be the inventor of the World Wide Web. W3C specifications are respected and, for the most part, followed by practically every software company, from Sun to Microsoft to IBM.

The W3C collects and publishes research reports in many technical fields, from e-commerce to graphics to languages. These reports are gradually refined and eventually published as formal recommendations for industry to follow. HTML, which sparked widespread use of the Internet, is perhaps the most well known W3C specification. A full list of the W3C's technical reports may be found at http://www.w3.org/TR.

The W3C does not actually develop products. However, most companies agree to use the W3C standards as a basis for building products such as web browsers, DOM and SAX parsers, and other XML tools.

The XML Recommendation and SGML

The W3C's XML 1.0 Recommendation, released on February 10, 1998 (and republished as a second edition on October 6, 2000), provided a drastic simplification of an older technology called Standard Generalized Markup Language (SGML). SGML is a complex standard for structuring, arranging, and representing very large amounts of information.

XML was designed as a developer-friendly, stripped-down version of SGML. The intent of XML was originally to provide for *program-*

friendly data over the Internet, a counterpart to the *human*-friendly and browser-friendly HTML standard also derived from SGML.

To see how the need for a program-friendly data format like XML came about, consider writing a program to extract a specific stock price from a web page. HTML mixes data (your stock price) with formatting information that describes to the browser how the page should be displayed. Extracting a stock price has traditionally involved *screen scraping,* that is, the parsing of an HTML document in a search for meaningful data that, unfortunately, has no identifier.

The stock price we want may be in a table between <TD> and </TD> tags, or perhaps stand alone on a new line between two <p> tags. Either way, HTML's mixing of the *data* (the stock price) with *presentation* (table tags, styles, etc.) forces us to first figure out where, graphically, our data is! Only when we know that our data is in the first row of a table or to the left of the banner ad can we write a proprietary program designed to seek out just that bit of data. Of course, should the web page format be changed by the webmaster, our program will cease to function.

The latest set of W3C standards simplifies the developer's world by actually encouraging a three-way split; *data* in XML (Chapter 3), *styling* in CSS (Chapter 4), and *document structure* in XHTML CN XM000103. The recent recommendation for XML schemas (Chapter 8) helps even more; in the example above, an XML schema might be used to ensure the stock price is numerical.

SUMMARY

Today XML can be found in almost every corner of the computing world. The surface has barely been scratched on the applicability of XML-related technologies. In fact, XML provides the underpinnings for an entire new generation of software, from Java peer-to-peer to Microsoft .NET.

Because of the extensibility of its grammar and its universal convenience, XML is taking its place alongside Unicode and TCP/IP as a critical, ubiquitous part of the computing world.

Chapter 2

INSTALLATION

A wide variety of applications exist for manipulating and viewing XML. This chapter illustrates the processes involved in the acquisition and installation of the various XML tools that will be needed for the explanations and examples that appear throughout this CodeNote.

HARDWARE

XML was designed for very general use, and as such it imposes few hardware requirements. XML parsers are available for almost all server platforms. Stripped-down XML parsers are even available for handheld devices such as the Java KVM, Palm OS, and Windows CE.

THE PLAN

All the technologies discussed in this book—XML, XSLT, DOM, etc.—are defined in *specifications* published by the World Wide Web Consortium (W3C, http://www.w3.org). The sole exception is SAX, which is maintained by a former W3C member named David Megginson. Note that the W3C does not provide actual implementations of these specifications. Generally, you must acquire and install implementations from third-party organizations, such as Microsoft and Sun. Usually these products are free and are often bundled together with other software (such as browsers).

The sections in this chapter will describe the installation and configuration of various XML and XML-related toolsets used in this CodeNote. These sections include:

- **XML Parsers.** XML parsers are APIs used to read XML files. Your platform probably already has at least one built-in parser; most major web browsers include one. This section will describe the installation of more application-specific parsers, for use with DOM (Chapter 6) and SAX (Chapter 7).
- **XSLT Processors.** Extensible Stylesheet Language Transformations (XSLT) processors are required for transforming XML with XSLT and XPath (Chapter 5). XSLT stylesheets are used to transform one XML document into another XML document, or can be used to translate XML documents to HTML and other nonstandard grammars.

You do not need to install both of these packages to get started with XML. In fact, if you already have a major browser (i.e., Netscape, Internet Explorer, or Opera) on your system, you may feel free to skip to Chapter 3 (XML Essentials), and return to this section if you need to set up additional components.

INSTALLATION PROCEDURES

XML Parsers

An XML parser is a utility, often accessed by a corresponding API, that performs the task of reading XML documents. Some applications, such as the SAXON XSLT utility described in the XSLT Processors section below, have private, built-in XML parsers. More often, however, a parser is an independent library shared by many different applications. Parsers generally support one or both of two APIs—the Document Object Model (DOM) or the Simple API for XML (SAX). Parser libraries are also available for many different programming languages, like Java, Visual Basic, etc. In order to write a program that manipulates XML, you will need to install a parser that has support for the interface and language of your choice.

You will need the following two XML parsers in order to implement the examples shown in Chapters 6 (DOM) and 7 (SAX).

Sun JAXP (Java)

JAXP is a Java API for processing XML documents, using DOM, SAX, and XSLT. JAXP includes a built-in XML parser, but will allow you to use an external parser as well. The examples in Chapters 6 and 7 all use JAXP and its built-in parser, so it must be installed on your system for those examples to run. Follow these instructions to install and configure JAXP:

1. Download JAXP 1.1 or later from http://java.sun.com/xml/xml_jaxp.html.
2. Extract the JAXP .zip file to a directory of your choice on your system.
3. Add `jaxp.jar` and `crimson.jar` to your CLASSPATH variable. To do this in Windows 2000 or NT4, first go to your Control Panel and select System. Click the Advanced tab, and click the Environment Variables button. If the CLASSPATH user variable does not exist, click New, and enter CLASSPATH as the Variable Name. Otherwise, click Edit. Add the full paths and filenames of `jaxp.jar` and `crimson.jar` to the Variable Value.

   To set the CLASSPATH variable from the command prompt, go to any command prompt and type

```
set CLASSPATH =%CLASSPATH%;c:\<your install dir>\jaxp.jar
```

   where `c:\<your install dir>\` is the full directory location of the `jaxp.jar`. Do the same with `crimson.jar`. This will change the CLASSPATH only for that command prompt. If you close it and start a new one the CLASSPATH will not be saved.

Microsoft MSXML (Win32)

As of this writing, MSXML 3.0 is the latest release of Microsoft's XML Parser. It MSXML3 provides a complete COM (Component Object Model) implementation of XSLT, XPATH, DOM, and SAX, usable from any Microsoft development environment and language. MSXML3 is required for the VB/COM examples in this book, including those in Chapters 6 (Programming with DOM) and 7 (Programming with SAX). To install and configure MSXML 3.0:

1. Download MSXML 3.0 Service Pack 1 (`msxml3sp1.exe`) or later from http://msdn.microsoft.com/xml/default.asp. Note that although it is termed a Service Pack, `msxml3sp1.exe` includes the entire MSXML package.
2. Run `msxml3sp1.exe` to install MSXML 3.0.

If MSXML 4.0 is available instead, install that version instead of 3.0. MSXML 4.0 will add support for XML schemas (Chapter 8) and perhaps other standards, though the code in the CodeNote will run unaffected.

In order for Microsoft-enabled applications such as IE, Outlook, and MSXSL (the command-line XSLT processor explained in the XSLT Processors section below) to use the newest version of MSXML, you should install MSXML in "replace mode." The following steps are required to perform a replace mode install:

1. Download `msxmlinst.exe` CN XM000101
2. Type the following on the command-line (`xmlInstDownload Directory` is the directory where xmlinst.exe is located).

```
xmlinstDownloadDirectory\xmlinst -u
```

If you have applications that require MSXML running, you will be required to close them before continuing. If any of these applications are running when you attempt to run `xmlinst` you will receive a warning message telling you which programs you need to shut down.

3. Register the MSXML dll with the following command:

```
regsvr32 msxml3.dll
```

4. From the command line, type the following:

```
xmlinstDownloadDirectory\xmlinst
```

XSLT Processors

To transform XML to another XML format or a non-XML format (for example, translating an XML file to an HTML page), you'll need an *XSLT processor.* Sun's JAXP and Microsoft's MSXML both include built-in XSLT support, so if you have these components installed, you do not need to install another stand-alone XSLT utility. You will need an XSLT processor for the examples shown in Chapter 5 of this CodeNote. The following are some suggested XSLT processors.

Sun JAXP (Java)

JAXP is a Java API that includes XSLT support as well as DOM and SAX support. To configure your system for using JAXP with XSLT:

1. Install and configure JAXP as detailed in the previous section, "XML Parsers."
2. Add the full path and filename of `xalan.jar` to your CLASSPATH user variable. For details on how to do this, see step 3 of the JAXP installation in "XML Parsers."

Microsoft MSXML (Win32)

XSLT support is provided with MSXML 3.0 by COM objects within `msxml3.dll` and dependencies. You do not need to configure your system any further to use MSXML's XSLT support.

MSXML's command-line XSLT support is provided by a utility called MSXSL, a link to which may be found at CN XM000101. In order to use MSXSL, you need to have installed MSXML in replace mode, as detailed in the previous section.

The SAXON XSLT Processor (Java and Win32)

Michael Kay's SAXON is one of the earliest XSLT 1.0–compliant processors, and it includes its own embedded XML SAX parser. Both Java and Windows versions are available from http://users.iclway.co.uk /mhkay/saxon/.

Download Full Saxon for Java development. You will need to place `saxon.jar` (included only with the Full Saxon download) in your CLASSPATH user variable. For details on how to do this, see step 3 of the JAXP installation in "XML Parsers."

If you are not planning to develop with Saxon, and simply want a stand-alone Win32 XSLT processor to perform XML translations via command line, you can download Instant Saxon. This utility is usable from the command line. The command-line interface of Instant Saxon is extremely useful for implementing the examples in Chapter 5 of this CodeNote.

XML Schema Validator

XSV is a command-line XML validator that supports XML schemas. You can download XSV as a command-line Windows application from the Language Technology Group CN XM000101. Simply download and run the self-extracting executable to install XSV. Solaris and Linux versions of XSV are expected to be available shortly.

You may also want to take advantage of the online, web-based version of XSV located at http://www.w3.org/2001/03/webdata/xsv. This version allows you to cut and paste your XML schema into a text box and validate it online.

Chapter 3

XML ESSENTIALS

Extensible Markup Language (XML) is a way of presenting structured information in a text document. It was originally created by the W3C as a recommended standard for displaying structured documents over the Web. XML has now been adapted for use in a variety of fields, from mathematics to health care.

XML is a refined form of the Standard Generalized Markup Language (SGML), which is a longtime standard for maintaining vendor- and system-independent structured data. Both XML and SGML use "tags" to mark up documents in order to provide structure. SGML predates the modern Web, however, and is much too complicated for browsers and web applications to conveniently handle. XML simplifies or eliminates many SGML features, making it a much more feasible option for web-based applications dealing with structured documents.

Hypertext Markup Language (HTML) is also a refinement of SGML, meant specifically for designing and displaying web pages. HTML is not useful for structured documents, however, because its semantics are fixed. Browsers recognize a certain set of HTML tags based on a current standard but will ignore tags that are not part of this set. XML has no predefined rules. It allows you to define your own sets of tags.

In a sense, XML is a "meta-markup" language, because it can actually be used to define markup grammars. For example, HTML can be (and has been) defined using XML. (See "XHTML" at CodeNotes Pointer CN XM000103 for details.)

This section will cover the basics of XML structure. After having read it, you should understand the theory behind XML, the parts of an XML document, and the manner in which XML documents are formed.

SIMPLE APPLICATION

The following is a simple, well-formed XML document. It holds a listing of tools (each tool denoted by the `<item>` tag) and describes each item with an identifier (`id`) attribute:

```
<?xml version="1.0"?>
<tools>
  <item id="3453">Hammer</item>
  <item id="1588">Screwdriver</item>
  <item id="8933">Monkey Wrench</item>
</tools>
```

Listing 3.1 A simple XML document

CORE CONCEPTS

XML Goals

XML was designed with several goals in mind, the most important of which are:

- **Simplicity**—XML documents should be strictly and simply structured, and should contain no features that are not universally recognized by all XML-supporting applications.
- **Compatibility**—XML is platform-independent. XML documents should be supported by a wide variety of applications. It should be easy to write new applications that make use of XML. It should also be easy to update existing applications to implement XML functionality.
- **Legibility**—XML documents should be human-readable. That is, the structure of the document and the meaning of its contents should be immediately clear to any reasonably computer-literate reader.

Viewing and Editing XML Documents

XML is text. XML documents can be read and edited with any software that will open standard text files. This means that you can use Notepad, vi, Microsoft Word, or any other text editor to edit XML files manually. Because XML is such a verbose language, however, it is often more desirable to work with software specifically intended for XML documents. Many such applications are available, including the following:

- **Altova XML Spy 3.5** is a complete development environment for XML that allows creation, validation, and customization of XML documents, XSLT (Chapter 5), CSS stylesheets (Chapter 4), DTDs (this chapter), and XML schemas (Chapter 8). The XML Spy editor allows multiple views of XML documents, including a color-coded text editor and a tree-based graphical view. Unfortunately, XML Spy is available only on Windows environments.
- **SoftQuad XMetaL 2.1** is an XML and SGML editor with DTD support. Its word processor–like editor allows you to view XML documents from a variety of different perspectives, including plain-text and tag-free. XMetaL is another Windows-only application.
- **ChannelPoint Merlot 1.0.1** is an open-source Java application for creating and editing XML. Merlot is a simple tree-based XML editor; however, plug-ins for editing DTDs and XSLT stylesheets are available on the Merlot website. One advantage of this editor is that it is platform-independent and should run on any operating system.
- **Microsoft XML Notepad beta 1.5** is a limited XML editor. XML Notepad does not support processing instructions or the creation of DTDs.
- **Tibco Turbo XML 2.1** provides excellent support for DTDs and schemas (including a very good visual interface). When developing an XML file according to a DTD or schema, Turbo XML provides error messages detailing that which is missing from the document. It also comes with short and effective tutorials.

All of these products are open-source or have free trial versions. If you want a full XML development environment with wide-ranging support for XML technologies, Altova XML Spy is probably the best choice at the time of this writing, and it has been used to design many of the XML samples in this CodeNote. Updated links to these applications can be found on the CodeNotes website CN XM000301.

Most of the major Internet browsers will also display XML, usually in very different ways. For example, whereas Netscape and Opera simply show the character content of an XML document's elements, Internet Explorer uses a built-in XSLT stylesheet to display the information in a color-coded expandable tree.

Topic: Basic Syntax

When we convert data into XML, we say the data is being *structured,* or *marked up.* This section will cover basic XML syntax for marking up data and provide some key definitions that will be used throughout the rest of this CodeNote.

CONCEPTS

XML Documents

An XML document consists entirely of text. The text can be either *markup* or *character data* (sometimes called parsed character data, or PCDATA). Generally, markup takes the form of *tags* that are used to structure the XML document. Character data is the information being structured (i.e., the text between the tags). Every XML document contains exactly one *root element.* The root element is the tag that appears at the beginning and end of an XML document, inside of which all the other tags are nested.

An XML document may also contain a *prolog,* which is simply text that appears before the root element. The prolog is usually used for instructions that are not part of the structured data, such as compiler directives, or a reference to a specific grammar. Listing 3.2 demonstrates a basic XML document with a prolog and a root element. Prologs will be discussed further in the XML Declaration section of the Other XML Syntax topic later in this chapter.

```
<?xml version="1.0" encoding="UTF-16" standalone="yes"?>

<root>
  <tag>Parsed Character Data</tag>
</root>
```

Listing 3.2 A basic XML document

Elements

Elements are the primary organizational devices for XML documents. You can think of elements as containers that hold and organize the information in your document. Each element must have a *start-tag* (e.g., `<tag>`) and a matching *end-tag* (e.g., `</tag>`) that indicate where it begins and ends. The end-tag name must match the start-tag name exactly, with the addition of a "/" character. Between their start- and end-tags, elements may have any combination of character data and other elements. Elements that contain both other elements and text are called *mixed-content* elements.

In the following sample, `<simple_element>`, `<tag1>`, `<tag2>`, and `<some_element>` are all basic elements, while `<a_mixed_element>` is a mixed-content element:

```
<simple_element>Character data</simple_element>
<some_element>
  <tag1>Some more</tag1>
  <tag2>character data</tag2>
</some_element>
<a_mixed_element>Even <x>more</x> character data
</a_mixed_element>
```

Listing 3.3 Simple and mixed-content elements

In this CodeNote, we will often refer to relationships among elements, so it is important that you understand the terms used to define XML relationships. When we refer to an *element,* we are referring to the entire element, including the start-tag, any content, and the end-tag. In the example above, we say that `<some_element>` is a *parent* of `<tag1>`, and that `<a_mixed_element>` is a parent of `<x>`. Conversely, `<tag1>` and `<x>` are *children* of `<some_element>` and `<a_mixed_element>`, respectively. The elements `<tag1>` and `<tag2>` are *siblings.*

We will also sometimes refer to *descendants* and *ancestors* of elements. Descendants of an element include all of its children, and the children of those children, and so on, ad infinitum. Ancestors are exactly the opposite; ancestors of an element include its parent, its parent's parent, and so on.

You will see in later chapters that it is often useful to have elements that contain neither character data nor other elements. These are called *empty-element* tags, and can be created simply by adding the "/" character to the end of a start-tag. Empty-element tags do not need end-tags.

```
<empty_element_tag />
```

Listing 3.4 An empty element

Empty elements are often used as place holders or to provide specific instructions inside an XML document. For example, XHTML uses empty-element tags for common formatting instructions such as a line break (`<br/>`).

Always remember the following properties of element names:

- They are case sensitive.
- They cannot contain spaces.
- They cannot start with the letters "xml," regardless of the case combination.
- They can only start with letters or the "_" character.
- They can contain numbers, "-", and "." in any position except the first character.

Attributes

Attributes are name-value pairs listed inside element start-tags. Elements can contain zero or more attributes, but the attribute names must be unique within an element. For example, you can't have two attributes named `index` inside an element's start-tag. Attributes cannot appear in end-tags. Attribute values must be enclosed in single (`'`) or double (`"`) quotes.

In the following example, the `symbol` attribute has a value of "ACME," and the `price` attribute has a value of "13.25".

```
<stock symbol="ACME" price="13.25"></stock>
```

Listing 3.5 Some simple attributes

Attributes are often used to contain metadata pertaining to the element, or to hold key values, but there are no firm rules. In fact, there are those who believe that XML would be better off without attributes, and that they are simply a legacy of SGML. Generally, anything that can be expressed using attributes can also be expressed using elements. For example, the `stock` element in the previous listing could be rewritten to use only elements.

```
<stock>
  <symbol>ACME</symbol>
  <price>13.25</price>
</stock>
```

Listing 3.6 Rewriting to avoid attributes

Like element names, attribute names are case-sensitive, cannot contain spaces, cannot start with "xml," and must start with either a letter or the "_" character.

EXAMPLE

The following XML document shows how elements and attributes can be used to create structured data on a collection of books. Note that the `<books>` element can contain multiple instances of `<book>`.

```
<?xml version="1.0"?>
<books>
  <book isbn="0812589041" genre="science fiction">
    <author>
      <firstname>Orson</firstname>
      <middlename>Scott</middlename>
      <lastname>Card</lastname>
    </author>
    <title>Enders Game</title>
    <year>1985</year>
  </book>
  <book isbn="0883853280" genre="biography">
    <author>
      <firstname>William</firstname>
      <middlename/>
      <lastname>Dunham</lastname>
    </author>
    <title>Euler The Master of Us All</title>
    <year>1999</year>
  </book>
</books>
```

Listing 3.7 Book list example

HOW AND WHY

How Do I Know Whether to Use Elements or Attributes?

Unfortunately, there is no good answer to this question. The argument concerning the usefulness of attributes in XML is ongoing. Many people feel that attributes are unnecessary and are simply a redundant feature in XML, inherited from SGML. Those who support attributes often quote the "metadata" argument, which dictates that you can put into attributes information that most humans and most applications won't need, in order to make it look better for the majority without removing the information altogether. In the end, it really does come down to appearance, and your personal preference. From a parsing perspective (as we will see in Chapters 6 and 7) elements can be slightly easier to retrieve and process than attributes; but these differences are rather insignificant.

SUMMARY

XML is a simple markup language that is easy to construct and easy to read. XML documents store data by two different means: elements (tags containing character data, other elements, or both), and attributes (name-value pairs placed within element start-tags). XML can represent any logical data structure using these constructs.

When using elements and attributes, always remember that both element and attribute names are case-sensitive and follow certain rules. Inconsistent capitalization is one of the most common (and painful) problems to track down when you are authoring XML documents.

Topic: Well-Formed XML

An XML document must obey a few simple rules in order to be syntactically correct, or *well-formed.* If you know HTML, many of these rules will be familiar to you. However, there are several major differences in what constitutes a well-formed HTML or XML document; not all well-formed HTML documents are well-formed XML documents. This section describes the rules that must be followed if an XML document is to be considered well-formed.

CONCEPTS

Start-Tags and End-Tags

Every element must have a start-tag and an end-tag. Elements such as HTML's `<br>` tag cannot exist legally in XML (although `<br/>` can, since it uses XML's empy-element syntax, demonstrated in Listing 3.4). Empty tags such as `<br>` are used in HTML for formatting or visual effects. XML is intended to be a structured *data* language, and, as such, has stricter rules.

The following is a well-formed fragment consisting of a start-tag, some data, and an end-tag:

```
<text>Some text here</text>
```

The following is not well formed, because it lacks an end-tag:

```
<linebreak>
```

Overlapping Tags

XML elements cannot overlap. Thus, the closing tag of a child element nested within a parent must appear before the closing tag of the parent element. This rule does not exist in HTML, where it is perfectly legal, for example, to have `<i>` tags carrying through multiple `<p>` tags.

The following fragment is a well-formed example of nested tags:

```
<para>This <ital>element</ital> is <bold>well-formed</bold>.
</para>
```

The following fragment is not well-formed because the `<bold>` element overlaps the `<ital>` element:

```
<para>This <ital>element is <bold>not</ital> well-formed</bold>
</para>
```

Root Elements

Every XML document must have exactly one root element. Documents with no root element, or with multiple root elements, are not well formed. In XML the root element can be any legal element name, whereas in HTML, the root element must always be `<html>`.

The following fragment is a well-formed, fully complete XML document:

```
<root>
  <data>Text</data>
  <data>More text</data>
</root>
```

The following fragment is not a well-formed XML document because it is missing a root tag:

```
<data>Text</data>
<data>More text</data>
```

Most XML parsers will reject this document with an error message about multiple root level nodes.

Attributes

XML attribute values *must* be enclosed in either single or double quotation marks. In HTML, it is legal (although not recommended) to have attribute values that are not delimited (i.e., they are not enclosed in quotation marks). Like HTML attributes, XML attributes must also be unique within a particular element.

The following is well-formed and uses double quotes to encapsulate each attribute value:

```
<element id="2" type="47">
```

The following is not well-formed. The first element is not well-formed because its `id` and `type` attributes' values are not encapsulated by quotation marks, and the second element is not well-formed because it has two attributes with the same name (`type`):

```
<element id=2 type=47>
<element type="46" type="47">
```

Illegal Characters

Character data in XML documents cannot contain "<" or "&". These characters have a recognized function in XML markup and are therefore reserved. If you want these characters to appear in your text, you must replace them with *entity references.* XML defines five entity references to provide escape sequences for the reserved characters, all having the general form `&referencename;`:

Reserved Character	Entity Reference
<	<
>	>
"	"
'	'
&	&

Table 3.1 XML entity references

In addition to the reserved characters, attribute values cannot contain, as printable characters, the same quotation marks with which they have been delimited. For example, suppose you have an attribute containing a quotation you wish to be displayed with the appropriate quotation marks, e.g., quote="Four score and seven years . . .". To include the quotation marks in the output, this attribute may be written quote='"Four score and seven years . . .'" or, using entity references, quote = ""Four score and seven years . . . "".

EXAMPLE

The following is a well-formed XML document. It has one root element, named <question>. <question> has one attribute, named instruction. Notice that the value of instruction has been delimited with single quotes, so that double quotes may be used within it. The second <content> element uses an entity reference to the "<" character such that the final line, if outputted, will display as 6 < 7.

```
<?xml version="1.0"?>
<question instruction='Press "ENTER" for the answer . . .'>
  <content>True or false:</content>
  <content>6 &lt; 7</content>
</question>
```

Listing 3.8 Well-formed XML showing quote differentiation and entity referencing

HOW AND WHY

Should I Use Single Quotes or Double Quotes?

It's really up to you. The important thing to remember is that if you use double quotes to delimit your attribute values, you must use single quotes within those values, and vice versa. If you want to use the same quotes within an attribute value that you have used to delimit it, you must replace them with entity references.

SUMMARY

In order for XML documents to be usable by XML readers and parsers, they must be well-formed XML. The rules for a well-formed XML document are simple and intuitive, if you keep in mind that XML is a structured data language. In fact, the rules can be boiled down to three basic statements:

1. Every start-tag needs a corresponding end-tag, and tags cannot overlap.
2. Encapsulate attribute values in either single or double quotes.
3. Watch out for reserved characters (< > & " '), and replace these characters with the proper entity reference.

Topic: Other XML Syntax

Although one of the goals of XML is to keep the language as simple and extensible as possible, several other features have been included to make it a fully functional markup language. These include the XML declaration (used to identify a document as an XML document and set other properties), processing instructions (syntax for including commands to programs that will parse the document), and comments (to keep an XML document readable).

CONCEPTS

XML Declaration

An XML declaration is used to identify a document as an XML document. The declaration is usually the first line of an XML document. While the XML declaration is not strictly required, it is usually a good idea to include it. If you do include it, it must appear in the first line of the prolog, before any comments, processing instructions, or the root element. A typical XML declaration looks like this:

```
<?xml version="1.0" encoding="UTF-16" standalone="yes"?>
```

The `version` attribute must always be included in the XML declaration, and will always contain the value "1.0" (at least until a new XML standard is released). The `encoding` and `standalone` attributes are optional but must appear in the order shown when they are included.

The `encoding` attribute allows you to specify how the text in your document is encoded. The value for this attribute depends on the manner in which your system encodes text, but the standard settings are either `UTF-8` (ASCII) or `UTF-16` (Unicode), either of which should work under most circumstances. Note that if you specify an incorrect or invalid encoding, your XML document may display incorrectly.

The `standalone` attribute indicates whether a document is dependent upon an external DTD (a "template" for XML documents that guarantees the document has a certain structure, described later in this chapter) or is an independent document. This attribute simply informs the parser that this document might depend on an external DTD. How the parser responds to this information is up to the parser author.

Processing Instructions

An XML file may include processing instructions (PI) with the intent that specific applications reading the document will interpret them as some type of command to be executed. Generally, PIs are used to inform the parser (most often assumed to be, but not necessarily, a browser) that it should associate the XML document with a particular XSL and/or CSS file. You may recall from Chapter 1 that an XML document may be associated with an XSLT and/or CSS file containing formatting information. Although we will cover this topic in the next chapter, the processing instruction to associate an XML document with a CSS file is:

```
<?xml-stylesheet type="text/css" href="mysheet.css"?>
```

The general format for a processing instruction is:

```
<?target instructions?>
```

Note that although the XML declaration discussed in the previous section (`<?xml version="1.0"?>`) may look like a processing instruction, it is not. It is a special, unique declaration used only to identify a document as XML.

Unlike the XML declaration, processing instructions can appear anywhere inside an XML document.

Comments

As in source code, comments can be included in an XML document to provide additional information about the document's contents. For example, you could use a comment to explain the structure of a particularly complicated element. An XML parser will ignore all comments, so they are entirely for the benefit of the human reader. If you know HTML, the format of an XML comment will be familiar to you.

```
<!--Here is a comment about something in the document.-->
```

You can put comments anywhere inside an XML document. However, you should be very careful to close the comment tag (-->).

CDATA

You can force text in your XML document to be treated as character data by enclosing it in a CDATA section. If, for example, you wanted an element to contain text with many illegal characters (raw HTML, perhaps), and you didn't want to replace every "<", "&", and ">" with an entity reference, you may want to leverage CDATA.

CDATA sections can appear anywhere within the root element of the document or its children, and can contain almost any characters, including those normally restricted by XML rules (such as "&" and "<"). A typical CDATA section looks like this:

```
<example>
<![CDATA[
  <html>
    <head><title>21st Century Technologies</title></head>
    <body bgcolor="blue"><p>Computers & More!</p></body>
  </html>
]]>
</example>
```

Listing 3.9 Using the CDATA tag

The text enclosed in the `<![CDATA[]]>` tags will display exactly as it appears in the XML, and all the tags and illegal characters in it will be treated as normal text. The only restriction on CDATA sections is that the combination `]]>` can appear only at the end of the section.

EXAMPLE

The following XML document (Listing 3.10) brings together all the various XML features demonstrated in this chapter. Consider building a help desk system for a government organization—the system collects problem reports from the field, encodes them as XML, and sends them to a central location for processing. Here is an example help request:

```
<?xml version="1.0" encoding="UTF-8" standalone="yes"?>
<problems>
  <problem title="Issue with &lt;storm&gt; elements"
    name="Rebecca D&apos;Angelo" id="3151" priority="low">
<![CDATA[
               Hi, it's Rebecca again.  There's a class 7
hurricane coming off the Atlantic seaboard, but the severity
element on the <storm> tag on only allows values of "small" and
"medium" and "biggie."  Can I submit a report with a value of
"mondo"?
]]>
  </problem>
</problems>
```

Listing 3.10 The storm.xml document

In an XML-aware browser, the output from this document would look something like this:

```
               Hi, it's Rebecca again.  There's a class 7
hurricane coming off the Atlantic seaboard, but the severity
element on the <storm> tag on only allows values of "small" and
"medium" and "biggie."  Can I submit a report with a value of
"mondo"?
```

Listing 3.11 The output of storm.xml

SUMMARY

In addition to elements and attributes, XML allows you to add XML declarations, comments, processing instructions, and forced character data (CDATA) to your documents. XML declarations identify a document as an XML document, whereas processing instructions (PI) are useful for associating an XML document with an external CSS or XSL file. CDATA blocks enable you to include a raw stream of characters in an XML file that the XML parser will ignore. CDATA is especially useful when you want to include raw HTML (or other markup) in an XML file, but you wish to avoid the task of replacing every < and > with an entity reference.

Topic: Namespaces

XML namespaces allow you to divide your structured data further into application-specific groups. Namespaces exist to overcome two complications:

First, most applications will concern themselves only with certain sections of your document. For example, if you have an XML document that describes restaurant franchises and employees, you probably have two different applications to handle franchise information (physical location, stock-on-hand, profitability, etc.) and employee information (name, address, salary, etc.). Namespaces allow you to indicate which information pertains to which application.

Second, namespaces help to eliminate collisions. A collision could occur if, for example, you had a `<name>` element describing franchise names (e.g., "McDonald's on 5th Ave.") and another `<name>` element describing employee names (e.g., "Bob Smith"). An application reading this XML could become confused because two entirely different types of data are using the same element name.

Listing 3.12 shows a very simple XML document that leverages two namespaces (store and manager) to distinguish between the name of a store and the name of the store manager.

```
<?xml version="1.0"?>
<resources xmlns:store="www.franchises.com/corp"
      xmlns:manager="www.franchises.com/hr">
  <store:name>McDonald's on 5th Ave.</store:name>
  <store:name>McDonald's on 6th Ave.</store:name>
  <manager:name>Bob Smith</manager:name>
</resources>
```

Listing 3.12 A simple XML document with two namespaces

This topic will describe how namespaces can be applied to elements and attributes in XML documents to allow applications easy recognition and to avoid collisions.

CONCEPTS

Uniqueness

The most important aspect of a namespace is that it must be unique. That is, unless you can guarantee that a reference to a namespace you are using will not be duplicated by any other XML document, collisions can still occur. Thus, namespaces must be identified by a unique Uniform Resource Indicator, or URI. Generally, when defining a namespace, you should associate it with a URI to which only you have a right.

For example, suppose you were creating a series of XML documents that contain product information for an e-store, http://www.shoppingis fun.com. Because you own this domain, you could associate your namespace with a URI such as http://www.shoppingisfun.com/product-info, which would guarantee that no one else would associate a namespace with the same URI.

Bear in mind that namespaces do not have to correspond to real URIs—they are simply unique strings. Thus, http://www.shoppingis fun.com/product-info does not have to exist as a real web page. It is simply a convenient string to use, and the fact that you own the domain should ensure that no one else will use it as a namespace.

Note that URI stands for Uniform Resource Indicator, and should not be confused with URL (Uniform Resource Locator), which is actually a *type* of URI, commonly identified by the HTTP protocol. Although most people do use URLs to identify namespaces, it is possible to use other types of URI as well. Therefore, this CodeNote will continue to use the term URI in its broader sense.

Declaring Namespaces

In order to include namespaces in your XML document, you need to declare them. XML namespaces can be declared within any element in a document, using the reserved attribute name, `xmlns`. A namespace will apply only to the element in which it is declared, and all of that element's children, until the corresponding end-tag for that element is encountered. In Listing 3.12, the `store` and `manager` namespaces declared in `<resources>` are valid for all child elements of `<resources>` until the `</resources>` tag is encountered. The scope and location of namespace declarations is further discussed in the Scope section at the end of this topic.

To associate an element with a namespace, we simply attach to the element name a *prefix* that represents the namespace. A prefix is really a kind of alias for the namespace string. Since a namespace can be long (and may contain characters not allowed in element names), we do not want to keep prepending this long string in front of each element that we want to associate with the namespace.

If, for example, you wanted to create a prefix `foo` to act as an alias for the namespace `http://www.stuff.com/foo`, you would have the following:

```
<text xmlns:foo="http://www.stuff.com/foo">
```

The code above declares that the namespace `http://www.stuff.com/foo` is associated with the prefix `foo`.

Any time a child element of `<text>` or an attribute of a child element of `<text>` is prefixed with `foo`, an application will recognize that that element or attribute is in the `http://www.stuff.com/foo` namespace. For example, the following XML makes use of the `foo` prefix to place `<word>` into the `http://www.stuff.com/foo` namespace.

```
<text xmlns:foo="http://www.stuff.com/foo">
  <foo:word>Antidisestablishmentarianism</foo:word>
</text>
```

It is very important to note, however, that `<text>` is *not* in the `foo` namespace. Just because a prefix is declared in an element does not mean that the element itself automatically becomes part of that namespace. To clarify, examine the following three namespace declarations:

```
1. <author xmlns="http://www.authors.org/namespace">
2. <author xmlns:aut="http://www.authors.org/namespace">
3. <aut:author xmlns:aut="http://www.authors.org/namespace">
```

The first defines a new global (default) namespace; the `<author>` element and all its descendants are automatically part of it. (Default namespaces are discussed in the next section.) The second defines a new namespace, but anything that you want to be associated with it must use the `aut` prefix, including the author element itself. The third does the same, but the author element is associated with the namespace. Note that its descendants still need to be explicitly prefixed with `aut`.

Default Namespaces

It is possible to associate elements with a namespace without using prefixes by assigning the namespace directly to the `xmlns` attribute. This technique is referred to as assigning a *default namespace.* For example, the following XML declares that `<people>` and all of its descendants (and its descendants' attributes) will be in the namespace http://www.mystore.com/people.

```
<people xmlns="http://www.mystore.com/people">
```

When you assign a default namespace to an element, all unqualified descendant elements of that element are automatically assumed to fall within this namespace. No prefix is necessary. In other words, you are assigning the http://www.mystore.com/people namespace to every single tag in the current scope (including, of course, the <people> element itself). If you want a tag to be part of a different namespace, you must explicitly prefix it. If you want all elements of a document to be part of a particular namespace, simply declare the default namespace in the root node of the XML document.

Prefixing Elements and Attributes

Once you have declared namespaces within an element, you can associate that element and any of its descendants with the namespace simply by prepending the element name with the prefix. Put another way, you can *qualify* an element with a namespace prefix to associate an element with that namespace. The combination of an element or attribute name with a prefix is called a *qualified name.*

To place an element in a namespace, add the prefix associated with the namespace to the element's start- and end-tags as shown:

```
<foo:person xmlns:foo="http://www.stuff.com/foo">
  <!-- details on this person -->
</foo:person>
```

Note that although you may read the contents of an element tag from left to right, a parser will read the namespace declaration before the element name. It is, therefore, possible (as shown above) for an element to be prefixed by a namespace declared to its right.

Remember to include the namespace prefix in the end tag; if you use </person> instead of </foo:person>, your document will not be considered well-formed. If two elements have the same name but are associated with different namespaces, they are considered completely different elements. <foo:person> and <person> are not the same element.

Attributes of an element are *not* automatically in the same namespace as the element in which they appear. In the following start-element tag, the attributes name and age are not in the namespace associated with foo, and will be ignored by an application looking only for foo prefixed elements and attributes.

```
<foo:person name="Frank" age="97">
```

You can associate attributes with namespaces by prefixing them. For example, the following element start-tag, <person>, places the element in the namespace associated with foo. The name attribute within this element is in the namespace associated with the prefix `bar`, and the `age` attribute is associated with `foo`.

```
<foo:person bar:name="Frank" foo:age="97">
```

Scope

The section of XML to which a namespace declaration and its prefix (if any) apply is called its *scope.* Namespace declarations can be made within any element. Namespace declarations, such as `xmlns:me="http://www.mysite.com"`, are available only to the element in which they are declared, and all of its descendants. In other words, the scope of this declaration encompasses only the element and its descendants, and only these entities can be associated with the namespace. If you attempt to use a namespace's associated prefix outside the scope of the namespace declaration, the XML may still be well-formed, but the prefixed elements will simply be considered stand-alone elements and not considered by the parser to be in the namespace.

Delving deeper into namespaces, the following XML document contains three namespace declarations but uses them imperfectly. See if you can identify a better way to arrange the namespaces:

```
<?xml version="1.0"?>
<cat:catalog xmlns:cat="http://www.books.com/ns/cat">
  <art:article xmlns:art="http://www.essays.com/def-ns">
    <art:title>Fun with XML Namespaces</art:title>
    <art:author xmlns:aut="http://www.author.org/namespace">
      <aut:firstname>Bob</aut:firstname>
      <aut:lastname>Smith</aut:lastname>
    </art:author>
  </art:article>
  <article>
    <title>Women in Shakespeare</title>
    <author xmlns:aut="http://www.authors.org/namespace">
      <aut:firstname>Sally</aut:firstname>
      <aut:lastname>Jones</aut:lastname>
    </author>
  </article>
</cat:catalog>
```

Listing 3.13 Demonstration of namespace scope

The `cat` prefix can be used anywhere in the document, because it is defined in the root element. The `art` prefix applies only to the first `<article>` element in which it is declared and will have no effect if used in the second `<article>` element. The aut prefix is declared twice—once in each `<author>` element. While this is technically correct, it would have been better to declare aut as a prefix in `<catalog>`, because it is reused throughout the XML document. In fact, any namespaces that you want to use throughout your XML document should be declared within the root element, so that the namespace scope encompasses the entire document.

If one were to modify the example in Listing 3.13 to use namespaces more efficiently, the `<catalog>` (root) element might be rewritten to look like this:

```
<cat:catalog xmlns:cat="http://www.books.com/ns/cat"
             xmlns:art="http://www.essays.com/def-ns"
             xmlns:aut="http://www.authors.org/namespace">
```

This declaration would allow cat, art, and aut to qualify elements anywhere in the document.

EXAMPLE

The XML document that follows in Listing 3.14 uses two namespaces. The namespaces used in this example are, however, special namespaces in that they are defined by the W3C for particular XML applications. XHTML and MathML are *grammars* of XML, and each uses a specific set of predefined XML element tags, which have been defined within the special namespaces http://www.w3.org/1999/xhtml and http://www.w3.org/1998/Math/MathML. Applications that recognize these namespaces will know how to handle the element vocabularies contained within these namespaces. The purpose of this example is to show a practical application of real, predefined XML namespaces.

```
<?xml version="1.0"?>
<html xmlns="http://www.w3.org/1999/xhtml">
  <head>
    <title>Namespace Example</title>
  </head>
  <body>
    <p>The ultimate question and answer, according to the late
Douglas Adams:</p>
    <p>
      <m:math xmlns:m="http://www.w3.org/1998/Math/MathML">
```

```
        <m:mrow>
          <m:mrow>
            <m:mn>6</m:mn>
            <m:times/>
            <m:mn>9</m:mn>
          </m:mrow>
          <m:mo>=</m:mo>
          <m:mn>42</m:mn>
        </m:mrow>
      </m:math>
    </p>
  </body>
</html>
```

Listing 3.14 Using standard namespaces (nsexample.xml)

XHTML is a revision of HTML designed to follow the stricter rules of XML. XHTML's grammar is extremely similar to that of HTML and uses most of the same element tags. In the example of Listing 3.14, the root element is `<html>`. The namespace declaration within this element says that all unqualified elements in this XML document are associated with the `XHTML` namespace at `http://www.w3.org/1999/xhtml`. Unqualified elements such as `<body>` and `<head>` will be recognized by any XHTML-compatible browser as XHTML elements, and will be handled appropriately (most likely, displayed as a web page).

The second namespace used in the example above is MathML. MathML is an XML grammar specifically designed for displaying mathematical equations on web pages. MathML uses elements such as `<mrow>` and `<mn>` to organize the equations, and these elements are associated with the `MathML` namespace at `http://www.w3.org/1998/Math/MathML`. In the example above, we associated the prefix `m` with the `MathML` namespace. We then qualified all MathML-specific elements with `m`, so that any browser that recognizes the `MathML` namespace will recognize these elements as `MathML` elements and know how to process them.

Note that our choice of `m` as a prefix is completely arbitrary; we could have used any prefix. It is the fact that this prefix is associated with the namespace URI `http://www.w3.org/1998/Math/MathML` that will enable any MathML parsing program to be able to interpret the mathematical data.

At the time of this writing, major browsers do not support XHTML or MathML.

HOW AND WHY

Do I Need to Be Online to Use Namespaces?

No. The namespace URI is simply a unique string, designed to ensure that collisions are impossible. Applications may recognize certain standard URIs, such as "`http://www.w3.org/1998/Math/MathML`," and automatically perform specific actions on the standard namespace tags. However, this functionality is built into the parser, and the URI is never actually referenced by anything.

What Happens If I Don't Prefix Elements?

If you have not assigned a default namespace, unqualified elements and attributes will be considered not to be in any namespace. Applications looking for particular namespaces will ignore unqualified elements and attributes.

Can I Reassign Namespace Prefixes?

Yes, although it is not recommended. For example, in the following code, the prefix `sto` is reassigned to represent a namespace for stock data, instead of store data.

```
<sto:store xmlns:sto="http://www.toolsrus.com/ns/store">
  <sto:name>Bob's Tools R Us</sto:name>
  <sto:address>123 Mulberry St.</sto:address>
  <sto:stock xmlns:sto="http://www.tools.org/ns/stock">
    <sto:item sto:quantity="50">hammers</sto:item>
    <sto:item sto:quantity="300">nails</sto:item>
  </sto:stock>
</sto:store>
```

Listing 3.15 Redefining namespace prefixes

It is generally recommended that you do not reassign namespace prefixes, as it confuses the meaning of the XML document's structure, and therefore goes against the principles of XML.

SUMMARY

Namespaces are unique strings that are used to avoid conflicts between different elements that may have the same name in an XML document. Namespaces also allow applications to recognize specific data subsets of an XML document and exclude others that they are not interested in.

A namespace may be associated with a prefix when it is declared. The prefix acts as an alias for the namespace, and by qualifying element names with a prefix, we associate the element with the namespace that the prefix represents. If you do not want to use a prefix, you can use a default namespace. A default namespace automatically includes the current element and all the descendants of the current element in itself.

Topic: DTDs

Document Type Definitions (DTD) are used to define the legal structure of an XML document. DTDs describe the structure, content, and quantity of elements, attributes, and entities that can exist within an XML document.

DTDs are useful for two reasons. First, they allow verification that an XML document is structurally consistent with a formal specification. That is, a group of XML documents can all follow the same rules in terms of the arrangement of their contents. Second, independent parties sharing a single DTD can be sure that the XML documents they create will share the same data structure.

DTDs are an application-independent way to maintain consistency among structured XML documents. DTDs are different from XML schemas, which are the W3C's recommended replacement for DTDs. XML schemas are covered in Chapter 8 (XML Schemas). Although schemas are likely to replace DTDs, there is still a good deal of DTD legacy in the industry, so it is important to understand them.

CONCEPTS

Validation

An *XML parser* is an API that reads the content of an XML document. A *validating parser* is a parser that validates an XML document against its related DTD, reporting an error whenever an inconsistency occurs. Programmatic APIs for manipulating XML documents, such as the Document Object Model (DOM) and Simple API for XML (SAX), can implement either kind of parser. These APIs are covered in Chapters 6 and 7, respectively.

At the time of this writing, most major browsers do not use validating parsers and will not detect validity errors in your XML documents where they are inconsistent with their associated DTDs. Internet Explorer and Netscape, for example, will display the contents of an XML document regardless of whether it conforms to its DTD. XML editors like XML Spy and XMetaL can be used to validate your XML documents against a DTD. Editors with validating parsers are discussed in the "Viewing and Editing XML Documents" section at the beginning of this chapter.

Document Type Declaration

DTDs must be declared with a Document Type Declaration. This declaration is generally placed at the beginning of an XML document to indicate that the document's structure will be defined by a DTD. DTDs can be declared within an XML document (these are called *inline* DTDs), or can be created as separate entities (files) and identified in the XML with an external URL reference.

An XML document with a Document Type Declaration for an inline DTD looks like this:

```
<?xml version="1.0"?>

<!DOCTYPE mydoc [
  <!-- DTD content goes here . . . -->
]>

<mydoc>
  <!-- XML content goes here . . . -->
</mydoc>
```

Listing 3.16 An inline DTD

The name that appears after `<!DOCTYPE` must always match the name of the XML document's root element.

To create an external reference to a DTD, use the `SYSTEM` command in the Document Type Declaration. External DTDs are more useful, because a single DTD can be referenced by multiple XML documents to ensure consistency.

```
<!DOCTYPE mydoc SYSTEM "http://www.mysite.com/mydoc.dtd">
```

The example DTDs within this chapter will generally assume that the DTDs are external entities.

Element Declarations

DTD element declarations allow you to define the contents of XML elements. You can indicate what child elements can occur within an element, and how many times each one can occur. The format for an element declaration is as follows:

```
<!ELEMENT element_name (element_content)>
```

The *element name* defines the XML tag for the element. The *element content* lists the names of allowed child elements.

For example, in Listing 3.17, we declare that every `<baseball_team>` element can contain an unlimited number of `<player>` elements (note the "*" that follows "player," meaning an "unlimited number of"), but only one `<name>` and `<city>` element. We then declare that each of these child elements contains only text.

```
<!ELEMENT baseball_team (name,city,player*)>
<!ELEMENT name (#PCDATA)>
<!ELEMENT city (#PCDATA)>
<!ELEMENT player (#PCDATA)>
```

Listing 3.17 Sample DTD

#PCDATA

PCDATA is shorthand for *parsed character data.* `#PCDATA` is the term used in DTDs to indicate that an element contains character text. For example, the line `<!ELEMENT name (#PCDATA)>` from Listing 3.17 above dictates that `<name>` elements can contain only character data and not other elements. The following fragment would be illegal in an XML document that references this DTD, because it includes subelements in the `<name>` element:

```
<name>
  <firstname>Bob</firstname>
  <lastname>Smith</lastname>
</name>
```

This, however, would be legal, as the `<name>` element contains only character data:

```
<name>Bob Smith</name>
```

Element Names

DTDs allow you to define both the child elements and the order of the child elements within a particular parent element. The children are listed in brackets within the element declaration, separated by commas. The line `<!ELEMENT baseball_team (name,city,player*)>` from Listing 3.17 says that each `<baseball_team>` element must contain `<name>`, `<city>`, and `<player>` elements, in that order. If a `<city>` element appeared before a `<name>` element in an XML document referencing this DTD, the document would not be valid.

Child element names can appear on their own, or can include one of three suffixes ("*", "+", or "?"). Element names without suffixes can appear only once within that element. In our baseball team example, the unsuffixed `<name>` element can appear only once in each `<baseball_team>` element.

Elements with a * suffix can appear zero or more times within an element. Our `<baseball_team>` can have one player, a hundred players, or no players at all.

Elements with a + suffix can appear one or more times. For example, the following declaration states that `<cast>` elements can have unlimited `<actor>` elements, but must have at least one.

```
<!ELEMENT cast (actor+)>
```

Elements with a ? suffix can appear zero or one times. This is useful for defining optional, but singular, child elements. In the following declaration, each `<name>` element must include a `<first>` and a `<last>` element, and may or may not include a `<middle>` element:

```
<!ELEMENT name (first,middle?,last)>
```

Choices and Parentheses

Your DTD can allow XML document creators to choose between multiple child elements using *choices*. A choice is indicated by the pipe ("|") character. For example, the following declaration says that `<clothing>` elements may contain either a `<pants>` or a `<skirt>` child element, but not both:

```
<!ELEMENT clothing (pants|skirt)>
```

You can also group child elements together using *parentheses*. This is useful if you want suffixes or choices to apply to multiple elements. The following declaration indicates that `<clothes>` elements must begin with a <glasses> element, and can then contain any number of <earrings> and <necklace> elements, in any combination or order.

```
<!ELEMENT clothes (glasses,(earrings|necklace)*)>
```

Mixed-Content Elements

Mixed-content elements can contain both character text and other elements. To define a mixed-content element, you must use a declaration like the following:

```
<!ELEMENT paragraph (#PCDATA|highlight|term)*>
```

Unfortunately, DTDs are not well suited to defining mixed content elements. For example, the above declaration states that <paragraph> elements can contain <highlight> tags, <term> tags, or character data, in any order. You cannot specify how many of each element are allowed, or in what order they are allowed to occur. For example, each of the following <paragraph> elements would be legal according to the DTD definition above (assuming <highlight> and <term> can contain PCDATA).

```
<paragraph>Why did the chicken cross the road?</paragraph>
<paragraph>
  To get to the <highlight>other side</highlight>
</paragraph>
<paragraph><highlight>Which came first</highlight>, the
<term>chicken</term>, or the <term>egg</term>?</paragraph>
<paragraph>
  <term>Chicken</term>
  <term>Egg</term>
</paragraph>
```

Listing 3.18 Mixed elements defined by a DTD

Mixed elements can be much more strictly defined using XML schemas, covered in Chapter 8 of this CodeNote.

Empty and Any

Empty elements are used for many XML applications such as XSLT and XML schemas, usually for specialized elements that only need to have attributes and no content. For example, XML schemas (which declare parameters for elements and attributes, just like DTDs) often use empty element tags to declare elements that contain only character content (PCDATA).

Your DTD can define an empty element with the following line:

```
<!ELEMENT shape EMPTY>
```

Conversely, you can also declare that an element may contain any content, element, or character data, using the ANY keyword. The ANY keyword is useful if you are defining an element for which you are not sure what the content might be, such as an <additional_information> element.

```
<!ELEMENT additional_information ANY>
```

Attribute List Declarations

DTD attribute list declarations allow you to define what attributes can appear inside element start-tags. In addition to defining the names of these attributes, attribute lists also allow you to define what type of value an attribute is allowed to have, and whether or not it is required.

The basic format for an attribute list declaration looks like this:

```
<!ATTLIST element attrib_name attrib_type attrib_default
                  attrib_name attrib_type attrib_default>
```

Although you can define an attribute list more than once for the same element, it is common practice to define only one, as each attribute list may contain an unlimited number of attributes.

Attribute Names

Attribute names must be legal XML names as defined in the Attributes section of this chapter. You can declare any number of attributes within an element, but each name must be unique in that element. The order in which you declare the attributes in the DTD is of no consequence, as they can be entered in any order in the related XML document.

Attribute Types

Attribute types can be used to restrict the values of declared attributes. For example, you could define an attribute whose value can only be a legal XML name instead of any character data. XML defines ten basic attribute types. Most of these are rarely used, because they are necessary only in very specialized XML documents. Examples of all ten attribute types are available on the CodeNotes website CN XM000302.

We will discuss four of the most basic attribute types here.

- ***CDATA*** attribute values can contain any legal XML character data. “34 Elm St.” is an example of a legal CDATA attribute value.
- ***NMTOKEN*** attribute values can contain only the characters legal in an XML name. One difference between an NMTOKEN and an XML name is that NMTOKENs can begin with numbers, dashes, or periods, whereas XML names cannot. “12943” is an example of a legal NMTOKEN attribute value. NMTOKENs are often used to prevent whitespace from appearing in attribute values, since whitespace cannot appear in a legal XML name.
- ***ID*** attribute values must be a legal XML name, and must be unique within the document. For example, suppose the `<employee>` element has an attribute `empid` of type ID. Each time `empid` occurs in the document within an `<employee>` element, it must have a unique attribute value. If you are familiar with relational databases, you can think of an ID as a primary key; it cannot repeat in an XML document, even if the `<employee>` element repeats.

  Note that because ID values must be legal XML names, it is not valid to have a number as an ID. Therefore, `empid="_123"` is legal, while `empid="123"` is not. This is an oddity that is overcome by XML schemas.
- ***Enumerated*** attributes are given a specific list of values that they are allowed to have. Enumerated values are enclosed in brackets and separated by pipes (“|”). This is a good means of forcing an attribute to use a restricted set of values. An example of an enumerated attribute declaration would be:

```
<!ATTLIST person gender (male|female|other) #REQUIRED>
```

Attribute Defaults

Each attribute declaration in an attribute list must indicate whether or not the attribute is required, and whether or not it has a default value. There are four possible *attribute defaults* in attribute list declarations.

- ***#Required*** indicates that this attribute must be included within the element in order for the XML to be valid. No default value is provided in the DTD, so the XML document creator must give a value for this attribute. For instance, the following definition states that every `<employee>` element must have an `empid` attribute.

```
<!ATTLIST employee empid ID #REQUIRED>
```

- ***#Implied*** indicates that this attribute is optional. No default value is provided, but there is no necessity to include this attribute. For example, the following definition states that `<employee>` elements can have `shoesize` attributes, but that the `shoesize` attribute is not required.

```
<!ATTLIST employee shoesize NMTOKEN #IMPLIED>
```

- ***#Fixed*** indicates that the attribute can have only one value, and that that value is set. The #FIXED keyword must be followed by a quoted string containing the permanent value of this attribute. The attribute value will remain the same regardless of whether the attribute is explicitly defined in the XML document. For example, the following definition says that the value of the `company_name` attribute of `<employee>` elements will always be `"ABC Inc."`, even if the attribute does not appear explicitly in the XML document.

```
<!ATTLIST employee company_name CDATA #FIXED "ABC Inc.">
```

- A ***literal string*** can be included in place of the above keywords to provide a default value for the attribute. This default can be overwritten within the XML document if the creator provides a value for this attribute. For example, the following declaration indicates that the `price` attribute will have the value "0" unless it is explicitly included with a different value in the document.

```
<!ATTLIST item price CDATA "0">
```

Entities

Recall from the Basic Syntax topic that XML defines five entity references to prevent certain characters from conflicting with reserved characters in the grammar (< > & ' and "). DTDs allow you to define your own entity references, which can then be used within related XML documents.

For example, suppose you were creating a DTD that would apply to a series of XML-based web pages, and you wanted to have the same copyright information on every page. You could create an entity reference in the DTD, assign it a certain name, and give it the appropriate XML markup for your copyright information as a value. You could then use this name as an entity reference in your XML documents whenever you wanted to include the copyright information.

The entity declaration might look like:

```
<!ENTITY copyright "<copyright id='123'><company>Bob&apos;s
Towing Co.</company><date>2001</date><copyright>">
```

You could then use this entity reference in your XML document, like this:

```
<footer>Copyright information: &copyright;</footer>
```

Note that quoted attribute values in the markup must use different quotation marks than those used to delimit the entity itself. In the example above, the entity value is delimited by double quotation marks, whereas the attribute values in the markup are delimited by single quotes.

External Entities

If you don't want to include the entire contents of your entity within your DTD, you can point the entity toward the location of an external file. This file becomes an *external entity.*

For example, if you had your copyright information in a separate XML file, `copyright.xml`, you could use the following entity declaration to reference it:

```
<!ENTITY copyright SYSTEM "http://www.mysite.com/copyright.xml">
```

Now, each time the `©right;` entity reference appears within an XML document referencing this DTD, `©right;` will be replaced by the entire contents of `copyright.xml`.

Using external entities can save you the headache of dealing with the different quote strings. It will also make your DTDs much easier to read and manage.

Parameter Entities

Parameter entities are entities that can be used *within the DTD.* Whereas normal entity references are accessible only from an XML document referencing a DTD, parameter entities allow you to define text content for repeated use inside a DTD. Parameter entities are particularly useful when creating extremely large DTDs.

For example, suppose you had a large number of elements with similar attribute list declarations, like this:

```
<!ATTLIST book  isbn CDATA #REQUIRED
                subject CDATA #REQUIRED
                genre CDATA #REQUIRED
                pages CDATA #REQUIRED>
<!ATTLIST essay isbn CDATA #REQUIRED
                subject CDATA #REQUIRED
                genre CDATA #REQUIRED
                words CDATA #REQUIRED>
```

Listing 3.19 Attribute lists with shared attributes

In order to avoid having to reenter the same information many times, and to keep the DTD cleaner, you can create a parameter entity to replace the repeated text. Parameter entity declarations look like normal entity declarations, with the addition of a "%" after the `ENTITY` keyword. Your parameter entity declaration could look like this:

```
<!ENTITY % refdata "isbn CDATA #REQUIRED
                    subject CDATA #REQUIRED
                    genre CDATA #REQUIRED">
```

You can then use this parameter entity to shorten your previous attribute list declarations by replacing the repeated text. Parameter entity references are preceded by a "%", instead of the "&" that precedes normal entity references. The following attribute-list declarations make use of the parameter reference we just defined:

```
<!ATTLIST book %refdata;
               pages CDATA #REQUIRED>
<!ATTLIST essay %refdata;
               words CDATA #REQUIRED>
```

EXAMPLE

The following DTD provides rules for an XML document describing the contents of a building.

```
<!ELEMENT building (floor+)>
<!ELEMENT floor (room*,washroom+,cafeteria)>
<!ELEMENT room (occupant|stores)?>
<!ELEMENT washroom EMPTY>
<!ELEMENT cafeteria EMPTY>
```

```
<!ELEMENT occupant (name, position, comments?)>
<!ELEMENT stores (item,amount)*>
<!ELEMENT name (#PCDATA)>
<!ELEMENT position (#PCDATA)>
<!ELEMENT comments ANY>
<!ELEMENT item (#PCDATA)>
<!ELEMENT amount (#PCDATA)>

<!ATTLIST building name CDATA #IMPLIED
                   address CDATA #REQUIRED
                   company CDATA #IMPLIED>
<!ATTLIST floor number ID #REQUIRED>
<!ATTLIST room number ID #REQUIRED
               size CDATA #IMPLIED
               rent CDATA #FIXED "300">
<!ATTLIST washroom number ID #REQUIRED
                   gender (men|women) #REQUIRED>
<!ATTLIST cafeteria number ID #REQUIRED>
<!ATTLIST occupant empid ID #REQUIRED

<!ENTITY comment_bad "Occupant is behind on rent dues.">
<!ENTITY comment_good "Occupant is paid up to present.">
```

Listing 3.20 DTD for XML documents describing buildings

We'll clarify the rules defined by this DTD:

1. Buildings must have an address attribute and can also have a name and company. Buildings must have at least one floor.
2. Floors must have one cafeteria, one or more washrooms, and any amount of rooms. Each floor has a floor number.
3. Rooms can have occupants, stores, or neither. Each room has a room number and may have a specified size. The rent on all rooms is 300, and this cannot be changed.
4. Washrooms have room numbers and genders. Washroom genders must be either "men" or "women."
5. Cafeterias have room numbers but cannot contain any data.
6. Occupants must have one name and one position. Occupants can also have comments. Each occupant must have an ID number.
7. Stores contain any number of items and amounts of those items, but if an item is included, the amount must be as well. That is, you can't have an item with no amount, or vice versa.
8. Comments can contain anything, including other elements. The

two entity references defined (`&comment_bad;` and `&comment_good;`) can be used to include generic comments for room occupants.

BUGS AND CAVEATS

Limitations of DTDs

DTDs are limited in terms of their control over the contents of XML attributes and elements. For instance, you cannot declare data types for elements, and the available data types for attribute values are not very specific. DTDs are also written in a different syntax than XML documents, and therefore cannot be parsed and processed by applications meant for XML.

XML schemas were developed because of these limitations. XML schemas are an XML grammar intended to replace DTDs as the standard for defining structured documents. Among other advancements, XML schemas provide forty-one standard data types (as opposed to ten) and the ability to define one's own data types. Schemas can express sets, can define limits on numerical element and attribute values, and can define substitutable elements. And XML schemas are XML documents, so they are readable with any tool that parses XML.

XML schemas are discussed in Chapter 8 of this CodeNote.

SUMMARY

Document Type Definitions (DTDs) define the structure of an XML document's elements and attributes, the order in which they can occur, and (within limits) the values they can contain. DTDs allow consistency among multiple XML documents and can be used to ensure that XML created by different applications in different locations conforms to the same structure.

Chapter Summary

XML is a simple markup language intended to be a platform-independent means of maintaining structured documents over the Internet. XML documents consist primarily of elements (start- and end-tags) and attributes (name-value pairs) containing character data. XML documents must follow a few simple rules to be well formed, and therefore valid. Namespaces in XML documents allow division of XML markup into application-specific blocks. DTDs define the structure of XML documents and can be referenced from each member in a group of similar documents in order to ensure consistency among them.

Chapter 4

—

STYLING WITH CSS

Cascading Stylesheets (CSS) are used to control the appearance of a structured document. CSS was originally conceived by the W3C to allow web developers and users additional control over how HTML documents were arranged and displayed. However, the CSS stylesheet syntax was designed in such a way that it can be applied to any markup language, including XML. In fact, since XML documents contain only structured data and no formatting or display information at all, CSS is the only way to tell web browsers how to display pure XML. CSS can make your structured XML documents presentable on the web.

To understand the rationale behind CSS, consider a large financial service corporation that uses XML to share records with its partners. Although XML documents are generally produced and consumed by server-side systems, we might often view this data directly in a browser—for verification purposes, for example, or for public display of certain XML data. Traditionally browsers display HTML files, often with the help of CSS, as shown in Figure 4.1.

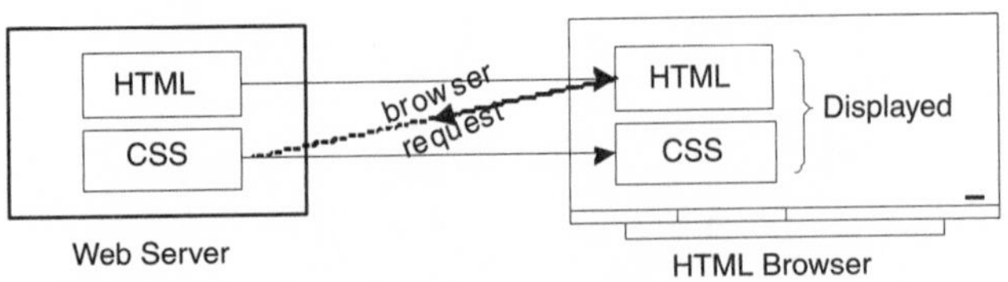

Figure 4.1 Styling HTML on the browser using CSS

The browser first retrieves the HTML file, and then retrieves the associated CSS file. However, the corporation's records are stored as XML, not HTML. We might go to the trouble of building a web server or application that converts our XML into HTML, but many browsers such as Netscape 6 and Internet Explorer 5 can actually render XML *directly*, as in Figure 4.2:

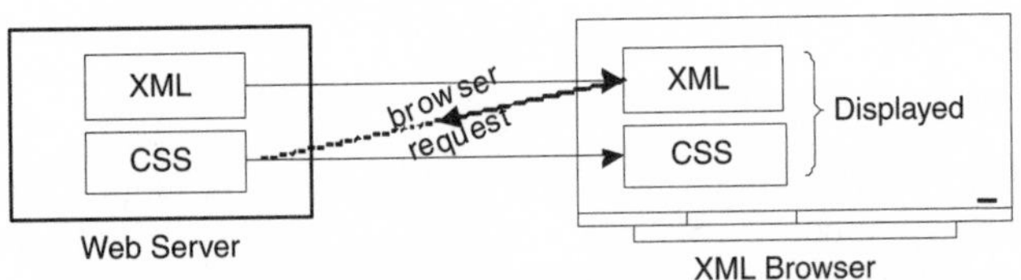

Figure 4.2 Styling XML on the browser using CSS

By linking an XML document to one or more CSS stylesheets, you may assign rich visual properties to elements and text, including background colors, borders, padding, and font faces. The CSS syntax used with HTML and XML are exactly the same.

This chapter discusses the latest W3C standard for CSS, known as CSS2. CSS2 adds new features to the original CSS, including internationalization, display characteristics that will inherit from parent to child elements, and the addition of tables. Unfortunately, CSS2 has not been fully adopted by the major browsers. Even now, three years after the W3C recommendation was released, support for CSS2 in Netscape 6, Internet Explorer 6, and Opera 5 remains uneven.

The full CSS2 specification may be found at http://www.w3c.org/TR/REC-CSS2/.

SIMPLE APPLICATION

First, let's see how an XML document displays in a browser without CSS. We'll use the following simple XML document:

```
<?xml version="1.0"?>

<document>
  <text>Hello World!</text>
</document>
```

Listing 4.1 Simple XML document

If we open this document with Opera 5, we would see just the unformatted text content of the elements.

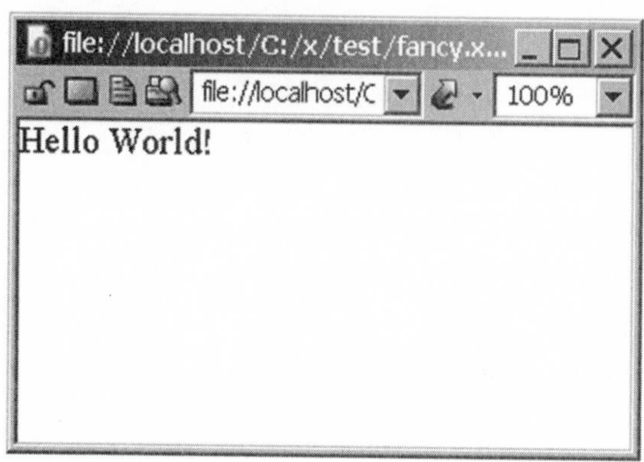

Figure 4.3 Opera 5.1 display of raw XML

Internet Explorer 6, left to its own devices, uses a default XSLT stylesheet to present the XML in a color-coded tree (XSLT is covered in Chapter 5):

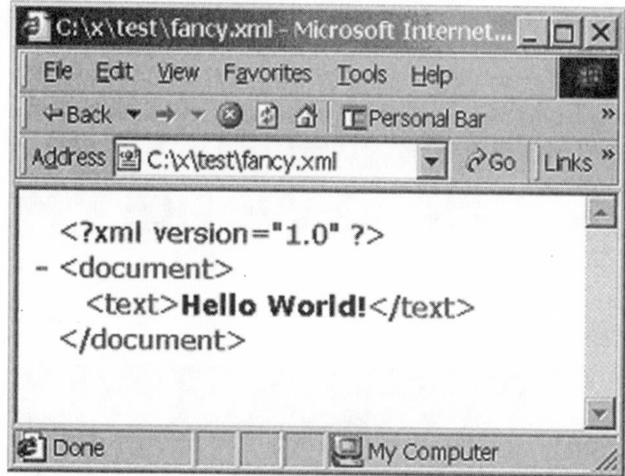

Figure 4.4 IE 6.0 display of raw XML

Neither display is very user-friendly. However, if we create a CSS file called `fancy.css`:

```
text {
  display: block;
  font-size: 48pt;
  font-weight: bold;
  font-family: Arial,sans-serif;
  text-align: center;
  color: blue;
  background-color: khaki;
}
```

Listing 4.2 Sample CSS file (fancy.css)

and add a processing instruction to our XML, directing all CSS-compatible browsers reading the file to style it using the supplied CSS file:

```
<?xml version="1.0"?>
<?xml-stylesheet type="text/css" href="fancy.css"?>

<document>
  <text>Hello World!</text>
</document>
```

Listing 4.3 Simple XML document with CSS processing instruction

we will see a much friendlier view. The document should now appear with the new display properties in any XML-capable browser—the Netscape 6 view is shown below.

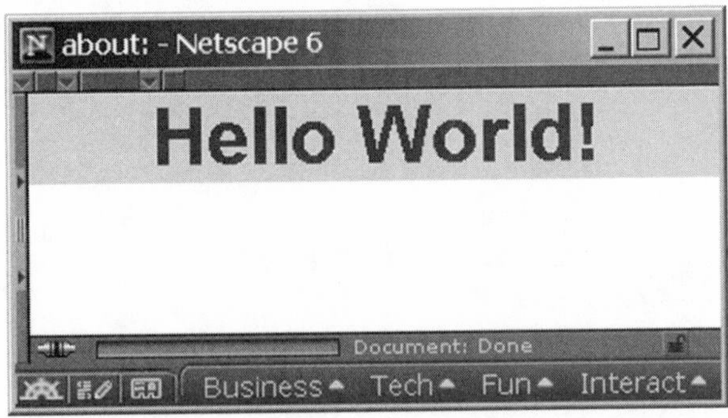

Figure 4.5 Netscape 6.0 display of XML styled with CSS

In many cases, CSS can allow you to create production-quality reports of XML data without resorting to creating full-blown client applications.

CORE CONCEPTS

What Is a Stylesheet?

Generally speaking, a stylesheet contains information on how to render a document. The CSS language can be used to style XML and HTML.

Stylesheets are deliberately kept separate from the source document—in this manner a stylesheet can be tailored for a specific device (such as a cellular phone screen) without affecting the document CN XM000401. Conversely, a stylesheet may be kept constant and applied to many different documents, to preserve a consistent visual format.

An example can be found in traditional HTML websites, where the hundreds of pages on a site will be linked to a small number of CSS stylesheets. By editing just these few CSS files, the appearance of an entire site can be modified.

Since XML is a data-oriented language, and contains no formatting tags whatsoever (unlike HTML), CSS is a natural solution for making XML documents visually presentable.

Topic: Selecting Nodes

Examine the following Cascading Stylesheet:

```
text {
  display: block;
  font-size: 48pt;
  font-weight: bold;
  font-family: Arial,sans-serif;
  text-align: center;
  color: blue;
  background-color: khaki;
}
```

Listing 4.4 A sample Cascading Stylesheet

You'll see that it contains no variables, loops, or any other programmatic structure. It simply declares how the `text` element is to be displayed, using a collection of name-value pairs. That's really all there is to CSS:

specifying expressions that match elements with visual attributes to be applied to them.

CONCEPTS

Linking XML to a Stylesheet

To style any XML document with CSS, simply reference a CSS file in the XML using an `xml-stylesheet` directive:

```
<?xml-stylesheet type="text/css" href="myStylesheet.css"?>
```

This reference should be placed *before* the root element and *after* the XML declaration. The `type` attribute indicates that the XML document is being linked to an external CSS file. The value of the `href` attribute should contain the URL of that CSS file.

Basic Element Selection

CSS stylesheets are made up of a series of *rules* that are matched against element tags in your XML document. Each rule is made up of an element name or names, and a set of any number of property-value pairs enclosed in curly braces (`{}`). The general format for a CSS rule is:

```
element(s) {property:value; property:value; property:value}
```

For example, if you wanted all `<title>` and `<subtitle>` elements in your XML document to be italicized and in a larger font, you might add the following rule to your stylesheet:

```
title, subtitle {font-size: x-large; font-style: italic}
```

The comma between `title` and `subtitle` indicates that this rule is being applied to both elements. Identical individual rules for title and subtitle would accomplish the same effect.

Note that the element names in the CSS stylesheet must match exactly the element names in the target document. For example, XML elements named `<TITLE>` or `<Title>` would not be affected by the above CSS rule. Inconsistent capitalization can cause major headaches when debugging large XML displays and should be carefully avoided.

The Wildcard Character

The "*" character acts as an element wildcard. If, for example, you wanted the contents of every element in the XML document to be navy blue on a khaki background, you could use the following rule:

```
* {background-color: khaki; color: navy}
```

The "*" character is useful for setting default display properties for a document's elements, which can then be inherited or overwritten by more specific rules.

Style Inheritance and Overrides

Specific rules may override general rules. For example, have a look at the following two CSS rules:

```
* {background-color: khaki; color: navy}
price  {font-weight:bold; color:seagreen}
```

If this CSS was linked to an XML document, the text within `<price>` elements of that document would:

- be boldface, as specified in the `price` rule.
- have a `khaki` background, inherited from the more general wildcard rule (the rule that begins with the "*" character).
- be `seagreen` in color. Though the wildcard rule contained the name-value pair `color:navy`, this rule was overridden by the `color:seagreen` declaration in the more specific `price` rule.

By using inheritance and overrides, you can quickly build an overall look for a set of pages, and then specialize particular elements as required.

Selection Operators

In addition to supplying rules for particular elements, CSS syntax contains operators with the ability to act on a set of elements at once.

The > operator selects all instances of a second element that are children of the first element. For example, the text of all `<poodle>` elements that are children of `<dog>` elements could be colored pink using:

```
dog > poodle {color: pink}
```

The + operator selects elements that immediately follow another. For example, the text of a `<color>` element immediately following a `<car>` element could be displayed in bold using:

```
car + color {font-weight: bold}
```

Remember that the + sign selects only elements that immediately follow others. If, in the linked XML document, a <car> element was followed by two <color> elements, only the first <color> element would be affected by the above CSS rule.

If you specify two element names without an operator between them, the rule selects the second element wherever it appears as a descendant of the first (as opposed to the > operator, which applies only to immediate children). For example, the following rule selects any <name> elements that are descendants of <employee> elements, whether they are children, grandchildren, etc.:

```
employee name {font-style; italic}
```

Attribute Filters

Although attributes cannot be displayed as text in browsers, they can be used to discriminate among elements.

For example, the following rule changes the background image of an element, depending on the (case-sensitive) value of the gender attribute of a person:

```
person[gender="male"] {background-image:url(xy.gif)}
person[gender="female"] {background-image:url(xx.gif)}
```

Attribute filters are very simple—you cannot combine boolean conditions, perform numerical comparisons, etc. You can, however, perform basic string searches, as illustrated on the CodeNotes website CN XM000402.

Note that the background-image property has highly variable support among the major browsers. Be sure to test against your target platforms, and be prepared to compromise beauty for compatibility.

Namespaces

CSS syntax has no knowledge of namespaces (covered in Chapter 3). Namespace prefixes are simply considered part of an element name. For example, you could use the following rule to format the contents of all <manager> elements in the namespace associated with the prefix corp, in boldface text:

```
corp:manager {font-style:bold}
```

Of course, manager tags that do not belong *explicitly* to the corp namespace (i.e., they are placed in that namespace by way of a default namespace declaration) will not be affected by the above rule. For example, an unqualified `<manager>` element (as opposed to a qualified `<corp:manager>` element) would not be affected by the above rule.

Conversely, if you were to create a CSS rule for `<manager>` elements, it would not be applied to `<corp:manager>` elements in the target document. Basically, CSS uses a literal string comparison on element names.

Comments

CSS stylesheets may be commented using C-style comments, as shown here:

```
/* colours below selected by Rob's design team, 11/5/01 */
// the above comment was written by a Canadian
```

Listing 4.5 Comments in CSS

EXAMPLE

Assume you generate or otherwise have access to a system log, formatted as XML:

```
<?xml version="1.0"?>

<log>
  <event priority="low"> <stamp>12:10:03</stamp>
      <msg>System started . . . </msg></event>
  <event priority="low"> <stamp>12:10:08</stamp>
      <msg>Order 279 received</msg></event>
  <event priority="high"><stamp>12:11:13</stamp>
      <msg>Order 274 denied!</msg></event>
  <event priority="low"><stamp>12:15:07</stamp>
      <msg>System shutdown…</msg></event>
  <!-- . . . -->
</log>
```

Listing 4.6 An XML system log

You could use the following CSS stylesheet to format this system log into a browser-friendly report:

```
log {font-family: arial, sans-serif; font-size: 8pt}
event {display: block;}
event[priority="low"] { color: green; }
event[priority="medium"] { color: yellow; }
```

```
event[priority="high"] { color: red; font-weight:bold; }
stamp { font-style:italic; }
```

Listing 4.7 A CSS stylesheet to create a report from a system log

We'll walk through this stylesheet line by line.

The first line in the CSS sets defaults for the entire XML document.

```
log {font-family: arial, sans-serif; font-size: 8pt}
```

The above rule specifies that, unless overridden by more specific rules, all character text within the log element will be in 8-point Arial font. One caveat to this is the comma that occurs in the `font-family` declaration—this comma implies that if a browser does not support the Arial family (which is unlikely), it will default to a basic *sans serif* font.

The next line specifies that each `event` should appear on its own line.

```
event {display: block;}
```

We accomplish this using the `display` property, which will be discussed in the next topic. For now, simply understand that setting `display` to `block` will force each event to appear in its own paragraph.

The next three lines in the CSS in Listing 4.7 color-code the different types of events based on their `priority` attributes. The last line italicizes the event times.

```
event[priority="low"] { color: green; }
event[priority="medium"] { color: yellow; }
event[priority="high"] { color: red; font-weight:bold; }
stamp { font-style:italic; }
```

Notice how we are using the attribute selectors (`[priority="low"]`) to specify the color-coding for the `<event>` elements in the document.

Once you have built the XML and CSS files from Listings 4.6 and 4.7, you can display the results in any browser that supports XML and CSS. Figure 4.6 shows the results in Opera 5. Note that, as of this writing, attribute selection has not been implemented in Internet Explorer 6, so the colors for different event priorities will not work in that browser.

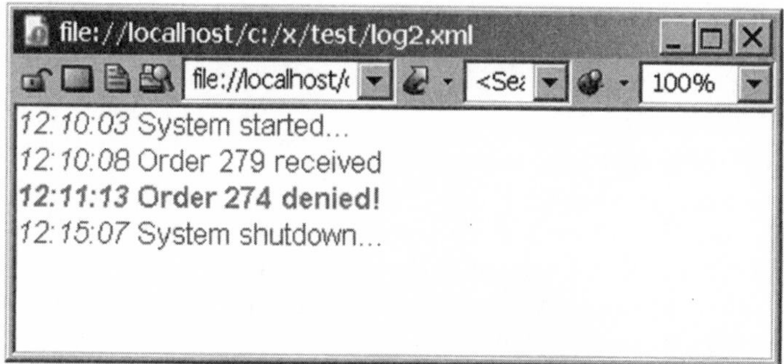

Figure 4.6 A CSS-styled XML log file in Opera 5.1

HOW AND WHY

Can I Link to Multiple CSS Stylesheets?

Yes. Simply specify multiple processing instructions. This approach is often used in large-scale situations. Many smaller CSS components can be built up into a CSS stylesheet for a specific task. For example, you could combine a basic stylesheet with a sales stylesheet to prepare a sales report:

```
<?xml-stylesheet type="text/css" href="base.css"?>
<?xml-stylesheet type="text/css" href="sales.css"?>
```

Listing 4.8 Linking to multiple CSS stylesheets

Stylesheets are applied to XML documents in the order in which they are linked. With the stylesheet tags in Listing 4.8, `base.css` would be applied first, and then `sales.css`. Rules in `sales.css` will override those in `base.css`, should they apply to the same elements.

When Should I Use CSS with XML?

You should consider using CSS with XML when:

- you are rendering static information in a browser that has both XML and CSS support, such as Netscape 6.0 and Microsoft's IE 6.0. For dynamic displays (e.g., collapsible trees) you will need to take advantage of DHTML or some other technology.
- the XML elements to be displayed are listed in display order (this is easy to arrange if you are generating the XML file yourself, perhaps from an ASP or a Servlet).

For example, a good candidate for XML and CSS might be a page showing the current state (up, down, offline, etc.) of a number of different system components.

Is XML Still XML When Linked to a CSS File?

Yes. The `xml-stylesheet` directive used to link an XML file to a CSS file is a *processing instruction;* processing instructions were discussed in Chapter 3 (XML Essentials). This processing instruction is read by applications deliberately attempting to render the document; all other applications will simply ignore it.

SUMMARY

CSS selects elements by specifying element names followed by a series of name-value pairs. Some of the important concepts to remember about CSS are:

- Element names in CSS rules must exactly match XML names in target documents.
- CSS supports both inheritance and overriding, which allow much greater formatting flexibility.
- You can apply one or more CSS stylesheets to an XML document using processing directives.

This topic examined how CSS selects elements for styling. The next topic will examine the most important name-value pairs, or properties, available for application to XML elements.

Topic: CSS Properties

CSS rules give you control over element *properties,* including font, colors, background images, margins, and much more. This topic will examine the most commonly used CSS properties and discuss their support in the popular web browsers.

Bear in mind when using CSS that your specifications are essentially requests, so you can't be sure that every application will display your XML exactly as you have specified.

The specifications below and in this CodeNote's reference card are a collection of the most useful attributes, though they by no means constitute an exhaustive list. You will find a more comprehensive list of CSS attributes at CodeNotes Pointer CN XM000403.

Also, as you work with CSS you'll find that many shortcuts exist for defining styles of an element. For example, the following `price` styles are equivalent:

```
price { font-weight: bold
        font-size: 8pt;
        font-family: tahoma; }
price { font: bold 8pt tahoma; }
```

Listing 4.9 Style shortcuts

Many CSS properties can be combined into a single all-encompassing property, with values separated by spaces to indicate the values of subproperties. In the example above, `font-weight`, `font-size`, and `font-family` are subproperties of the `font` property.

CONCEPTS

Colors

CSS exposes three color-related controls: `color`, `background-color`, and `border-color`. Each may be specified by name or a hexadecimal triplet, as in the following listing:

```
item { color: #F0E68C; }
quantity { color: silver; border-color: navy}
price { color: yellow; background-color: blue; }
```

Listing 4.10 Color properties

The reference card contains a list of the sixteen standard colors that are available in every browser. Browsers generally support an additional set of several dozen named colors from another specification, including `darkkhaki`, `mintcream`, and `seashell`.

The `background-color` property may also be set to `transparent`. When the `transparent` attribute is set, the background color is not displayed. This is useful if you don't want certain elements to override the background colors of other elements.

Backgrounds

In addition to `background-color`, several properties allow a bitmap to be used as an element background. The most important of these is the `background-image` property.

```
stock[action="b"] { background-image: url("buy.gif"); }
stock[action="s"] { background-image: url("sell.gif"); }
```

Listing 4.11 Background image properties

The above rules set `buy.gif` as the background for all `<stock>` elements whose `action` attribute equals "b," and `sell.gif` as the background for all `<stock>` elements whose `action` attribute equals "s."

Unfortunately, browser support for the CSS attribute `background-image` with XML is uneven. Always test your target platform.

Fonts

CSS provides rich control over the applied font. The most useful font attributes are:

Attribute	Use	Example Value
font-style	Used to set italics, bold, small caps, etc.	font-style: italics
font-weight	Used to set font weight (bold, light, etc.)	font-weight: bold
font-family	Sets the font-family name. Common fonts include Arial, Sans-Serif, and Times Roman	font-family: arial
font-size	Sets the font-size in points, or with a generic setting such as larger or smaller	font-size: 12
text-align	Sets the text alignment to center, left justified, or right justified. The default is left justified	text-align: center

Table 4.1 Font properties

Common values for these attributes are listed on the reference card.

The `font-family` property allows multiple font faces to be specified in case a preferred choice is not available. The last five values on the reference card are general families, and you may wish to specify one of these as your last fallback position.

For example, when applying the following rule, the browser would attempt to display `<footnote>` elements using the `tahoma` font family. If the `tahoma` family of fonts was not supported, it would try `arial`. Failing that, it would default to a generic `sans-serif` font, which every browser should have.

```
footnote {font-family:  tahoma, arial, sans-serif }
```

Font-size may take on many values. You can specify generic, relative values (e.g., `large`, `larger`, `smaller`) or absolute values (e.g., `10pt`). Remember that absolute sizes will not be portable across platforms.

Display

The `display` property determines how elements are arranged on a page. For example, element text can be displayed as inline text (i.e., no new line), paragraphs (i.e., on its own line), or as lists.

The default `display` value is `inline`. Elements displayed inline will simply be placed on the same line as the previous element, within the paragraph, list, or however the previous element happened to be displayed.

If the `display` property is set to `block`, the element will be placed on its own line as a "block" of text.

For example, consider the following two CSS rules.

```
para { display:block; }
special, neat, cool { display:inline; font-weight:bold}
```

If we took the above rules and applied them to an XML document like this:

```
<para>This element is in a block. The last word in this sentence
is <special>bold</special>. The last word in this sentence is
also <neat>bold</neat>. And finally, the last word in this
sentence is (you guessed it) <cool>bold</cool>.</para>
```

then the output (in Opera 5) would look like this:

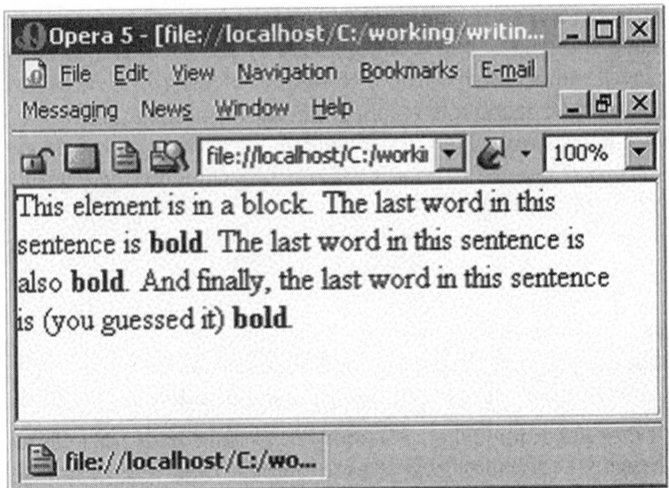

Figure 4.7 The display property

Element text may also be hidden from view completely using `display:none`. The following rule hides the text of all elements whose `secret` attribute has a value of "1":

```
*[secret="1"] {display: none}
```

Lists

CSS supports both bulleted and numbered lists. Any element whose `display` property is set to `list-item` will display as an item in a list. To indicate what type of list you want (bulleted, numbered, etc.), you need to use the `list-style-type` property. For example, the following rules could be used to create a numbered list of items (assuming that `<item>` elements are children of `<store>` elements):

```
store {display: block; list-style-type: decimal}
item {display: list-item}
```

Note that lists do not have consistent support in the major browsers.

Pseudo-Classes

Pseudo-classes are used to reference elements by their status, as opposed to their element name. Although the concept is useful, support for pseudo-classes as applied to XML is very scarce.

A common application of pseudo-classes in HTML is to control the colors of a link based on its state (for example, visited or not). XML support for linking is still in its infancy at the time of this writing (see

CodeNotes Pointer XM000104), but the CSS syntax will likely remain the same.

For example, if you wanted all visited `detail` elements to appear blue, you might use:

```
detail:visited {color: blue}
```

Another useful pseudo-class is `first-child`, which allows you to refer to the first element in a list of siblings. For example, the following rule selects the first child element of `<competitor>` elements in an XML document and increases its font size.

```
competitor:first-child {font-size: larger}
```

As of the time of this writing, only Netscape 6 supports the `first-child` pseudo-class.

Pseudo-Elements

A pseudo-element refers to a *subset* of an element's character data. With pseudo-elements you can define rules for text fragments that aren't explicitly marked up as XML elements.

before and after

The `before` and `after` pseudo-elements can be very useful. These two pseudo-elements allow you to include text that will appear before and after a particular element. For example, suppose you stored data concerning a book collection in the following manner:

```
<book>
  <title>Neuromancer</title>
  <author>William Gibson</author>
  <!--  . . .  -->
</book>
```

Listing 4.12 Sample book collection XML

To display each book as a sentence you might use a CSS stylesheet like this one:

```
book {display:block}
title:before {
  font-weight:normal;
  content: "I have read and enjoyed "
}
```

```
title {font-weight: bold}
author:before {content: " by "}
author:after {content: "."}
```

Listing 4.13 CSS to convert book collection data into sentences

In a browser, each book would be displayed on its own line, in the format: "I have read and enjoyed **Neuromancer** by William Gibson."

Notice that in the CSS above, we had to add the `font-weight` property to both the `title:before` and `title` elements. This is because `title:before` actually inherits properties from `title`. If `font-weight:normal` had not been added to `title:before`, its content would have been displayed in bold.

first-letter and first-line

The two other pseudo-elements are `first-letter` and `first-line`. These allow you to apply a rule to the first character or line of an element's text, respectively. Note that the definition of a "line" depends on the size of the browser window, such that `first-line` may refer to a greater amount of text in a larger browser window than it would in a smaller one.

For example, suppose you had XML with large quantities of text. To display the first line of each text block in italics, and the first letter of each line extra large, you might use:

```
text:first-letter {font-size: xx-large; font-weight:bold}
text:first-line {font-style: italic}
```

Listing 4.14 Formatting with first-letter and first-line

Pseudo-elements are not consistently supported across the major browsers. This table shows support in the most recent versions of these browsers:

	before	**after**	**first-letter**	**first-line**
Netscape 6.0	Yes	Yes	No	No
IE 6.0	No	No	No	No
Opera 5.11	Yes	Yes	Yes	No

Table 4.2 Pseudo-element support in popular browsers

EXAMPLE

In this example, we will take an XML document that contains header information and lines of text from a book, and apply to it a stylesheet that will format it in an attractive manner for the browser. We'll make use of most of the features described in this chapter.

Here is the XML document we will be formatting:

```
<?xml version="1.0"?>
<?xml-stylesheet type="text/css" href="book.css"?>

<book>
  <info>
    <title>The Canterbury Tales</title>
    <author>Geoffrey Chaucer</author>
    <date>c. 1400</date>
  </info>
  <chapter title="The General Prologue">
    <line>Whan that aprill with his shoures soote
    <footnote>1</footnote></line>
    <line>The droghte of march hath perced to the roote,</line>
    <line>And bathed every veyne in swich licour</line>
    <line>Of which vertu engendred is the flour;</line>
    <line>Whan zephirus eek<footnote>2</footnote>
    with his sweete breeth</line>
    <line>Inspired hath in every holt and heeth</line>
    <line>Tendre croppes, and the yonge sonne</line>
    <line>Hath in the Ram his halfe cours yronne</line>
    <!--More lines to come . . . -->
    <footnotes>
      <note>
        <term>shoures soote</term>
        <definition>sweet showers</definition>
      </note>
      <note>
        <term>eek</term>
        <definition>also</definition>
      </note>
    </footnotes>
  </chapter>
  <!--More chapters to come . . . -->
</book>
```

Listing 4.15 XML containing lines from a book (ctales.xml)

The above XML document contains some reference information on the book (title, author, date), the text of the book itself, and we've added some footnotes defining key terms in the chapter.

Now let's create a CSS file to format this document. We'll start by creating the file `book.css`, to which our sample XML is already linked (using the `xml-stylesheet` processing instruction). In `book.css`, we'll first provide default styling for the entire document using a style on the root element, as follows:

```
book {
  font-family: "Arial", sans-serif;
  font-size: small;
  color:black
}
```

Listing 4.16 The beginning of book.css (setting up default styles)

Next we'll add some code that will format the <title>, <author>, and <date> elements, so that they will stand out from the rest of the text:

```
info {display: block; text-align: center}
title {
  display: block;
  font-family: "script",cursive;
  font-size: xx-large;
  color: navy
}
author:before {color:black; content: "by "}
author {display:inline; font-size: medium; color:green;}
date:before {content: "("}
date {display:inline; font-size: medium; font-style: italic}
date:after {content: ")"}
```

Listing 4.17 Formatting header information in book.css

Notice that in the above CSS, we created a rule for the <info> element that centers the text. This rule will be inherited by all the other elements in this section, because they are children of <info>. Also, notice that the `before` and `after` pseudo-elements were used to provide additional content to the <author> and <date> elements.

Next, we'll specify styling for the text of the book fragment:

```
chapter {
  display:block;
  text-indent: 35%;
```

```
  position:relative;
  top:20px;}
chapter line:first-child:first-letter {
  float:none;
  font-size:x-large;}
line {display:block;}
footnote {
  display:inline;
  font-size: xx-small;
  vertical-align:super}
```

Listing 4.18 Formatting book text in book.css

The important thing to notice here is that we've used the `first-child` pseudo-class and `first-letter` pseudo-element, shown in boldface. This line applies the rule to the first character of the first `<line>` in the `<chapter>`, and makes it larger than the regular text.

Also, we've created a rule for the inline style `footnote` so that the text in these elements will appear superscripted and small.

Finally, we define how we want the footnotes to be displayed at the bottom of the chapter. We use the `before` pseudo-element to create a title for the footnotes section, and then format the rest as an ordered list of terms and definitions, to match up with the numbers in the text. The CSS code for this is as follows:

```
footnotes:before {
  text-decoration:underline;
  content:"Footnotes: "}
footnotes {
  display:block;
  list-style-type:decimal;
  font-size:x-small;
  position:relative;
  text-indent: 35%;
  top:20px}
note {
  display:list-item;
  text-indent:37.5%}
term {font-weight:bold; color:blue}
term:after {display:inline; color:black; content: " = "}
definition {display:inline}
```

Listing 4.19 Formatting the footnotes in book.css

Let's look at how Netscape 6.0 handles the styling we've applied to `ctales.xml`:

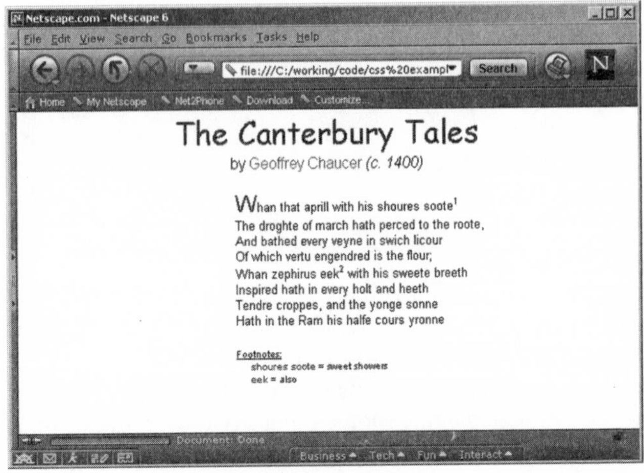

Figure 4.8 Netscape 6 rendering of CSS enriched XML (ctales.xml)

Netscape 6 does not handle the `list-style-type` correctly; therefore it does not show the footnotes as a numbered list. Other browsers will have different, but similar, minor shortcomings. For example, Opera 5 will list the items, but will number them incorrectly.

HOW AND WHY

Where Can I Find CSS Properties and Browser Support Information?

You'll find many excellent CSS references on the web XM000403. Often these references assume that you are using CSS to format HTML, however; XML/CSS may behave differently from HTML/CSS.

More advanced users may also want to look at the CSS Level 2 Specification, located at http://www.w3.org/TR/REC-CSS2/.

BUGS AND CAVEATS

Browser Support

The major caveat for CSS2 is, of course, inconsistent support. The major browsers have been slow and uneven in implementing CSS2 functionality. As always with web-based development, either you must have tight control over your users' browser options, or you must test on the range of browsers that might be used and trade features for compatibility where required.

DESIGN NOTES

What Is XSL-FO?

XSL Formatting Objects (XSL-FO) is a draft W3C standard for adding style information to XML documents based on a new XML grammar. (CSS is, of course, not an XML grammar, since it doesn't follow XML rules.) XSL-FO is not yet supported by any major browser. It is primarily intended to be an intermediate format for representing style information very precisely. For example, you might write an XSLT stylesheet to convert your XML document into an XSL-FO document with formatting information. You would then use a utility to translate the XSL-FO document into the target format you desire, such as PDF. It is unlikely that you will encounter XSL-FO in the near future.

SUMMARY

CSS attributes can be used to control the appearance of almost any HTML element. You can set attributes that affect color, font, text size, text alignment, list style, background, and many other properties. However, when you work with CSS properties, you should always keep in mind that CSS properties are requests made to the browser. The browser does not necessarily implement your instructions in the manner you specify. In other words, there is no substitute for thorough testing on your target platforms.

Chapter Summary

Cascading Stylesheets allow you to apply styling to XML documents in order to display their structured information in a web-based, visually appealing format. CSS stylesheets consist of rules that select particular elements or groups of elements and apply presentation information to them. XML documents can be linked to one or more CSS stylesheets using processing instructions. CSS rules consist of list of property-value pairs, each one controlling a different aspect of how an element displays (font, color, size, etc.).

CSS2 (the newest W3C CSS Recommendation) holds considerable power, but is unfortunately hampered by uneven support. However, the XML/CSS combination is still an attractive, easy alternative to more programmer-oriented rendering technologies such as Servlets or XSLT, especially where your target browser is restricted.

Chapter 5

XSLT AND XPATH

Almost any application that processes XML will find itself performing a *transformation* of some kind. One of the most celebrated and useful XML transformations (but by no means the only) is the transformation of an XML document to an HTML page for display by a browser. Extensible Stylesheet Language Transformations (XSLT) is the key technology that performs this and other transformations. XSLT can be used to transform any one kind of XML grammar (perhaps one that you define) to any other form of XML grammar. XSLT can also map XML documents to output documents that do not strictly follow the rules of proper XML grammar, HTML being one example.

To take advantage of XSLT, you don't program—instead you write rules, called *templates,* which are matched against elements in your input XML. The templates work by mapping XML tags and data from your input document to new and different tags of your choosing in an output document. XPath is a compact query language used within XSLT primarily for selecting nodes (elements, attributes, or character data) from the input XML. However, as you will likely first encounter XPath in conjunction with XSLT, we present them here together.

In Chapter 4 we examined another styling language, CSS. CSS should be used with XML when you want to create an XML-based web page that requires no forms, dynamic behavior, or other complex features. If any of these special properties are required, you should use XSLT to generate an HTML page, and then use CSS to style it. Detailed schematics outlining these architectures are presented later in this chapter.

A word of caution: XSLT is one of the more complicated subjects discussed in this book. However, its power and elegance make the struggle worthwhile, and once you have learned it you will likely find it indispensable.

References to the W3C XSLT and XPath specifications are available on the CodeNotes website XM000501.

SIMPLE APPLICATION

We will demonstrate a simple transformation from a custom XML grammar into HTML using XSLT. The resulting HTML file will be viewable in any web browser.

There are *three* players in any XSLT transformation: the source, or input XML; the XSLT stylesheet itself; and the resulting output document.

The Input XML

We begin by creating `data.xml`, for use as the input:

```
<?xml version="1.0"?>
<message>Howdy!</message>
```

Listing 5.1 XML input file (data.xml)

The XSLT Stylesheet

Next we create the `render.xsl` stylesheet, which will contain the rules, known as templates, which specify how to transform our source XML into HTML:

```
<?xml version="1.0"?>
<xsl:stylesheet
  version="1.0"
  xmlns:xsl="http://www.w3.org/1999/XSL/Transform">

  <!-- one rule, to transform the input root (/) -->
  <xsl:template match="/">
    <html><body>
      <!-- select message text using an XPath statement-->
        <h1><xsl:value-of select="./message/text()"/></h1>
```

```
    </body></html>
  </xsl:template>
</xsl:stylesheet>
```

Listing 5.2 XSLT stylesheet for transforming XML into HTML (render.xsl)

Despite appearances, you don't need to be online for this example to work—the namespace is just a unique string that declares that this file is XSLT; the URI is never resolved.

Generating Output

Before running the transformation, first verify that both `data.xml` and `render.xsl` are valid XML documents as discussed in Chapter 3 (XML Essentials) under "Well-Formed XML." Also, select and install an XSLT processor as outlined in Chapter 2 (Installation). Then follow the appropriate instructions for your processor:

Sun JAXP (Java)

Ensure `xalan.jar` is in your `CLASSPATH` system variable, open a command prompt, and type (as one line):

```
java org.apache.xalan.xslt.Process -in data.xml -xsl render.xsl
```

Microsoft MSXML (Win32)

From a command prompt run:

```
MSXSL data.xml render.xsl
```

Full Saxon (Java Application)

Ensure `saxon.jar` is in your `CLASSPATH` and run:

```
java com.icl.saxon.StyleSheet data.xml render.xsl
```

Instant Saxon (Windows Executable)

From a command prompt run:

```
saxon data.xml render.xsl
```

Remember that you will need to include full path information for the XML and XSL files if they are not in the same directory as SAXON. The output in all cases should be as follows:

```
<html><body><h1>Howdy!</h1></body></html>
```

Listing 5.3 Output of transformation

You may capture this output into a file for viewing in a browser using *file redirection.* To redirect the output, add `" > out.html"` to the end of any of the commands shown above. This will create a file called `out.html` with the contents of the final output HTML.

To review what we have accomplished: The XSLT processor used the transformation rules (specified in `render.xsl`) against a supplied input (`data.xml`) to produce the output shown in Listing 5.3. We may now convert any similarly encoded message into HTML using this process.

If you are using MSXML, you'll notice Unicode (two bytes per character) output instead of ASCII (you'll see what appear to be spaces between each output character). With any processor, you can manually force either Unicode or ASCII character output by inserting *one* of the following lines just above the first comment in `render.xsl`:

```
<xsl:output encoding="UTF-8"/><!-- output ASCII -->

<xsl:output encoding="UTF-16"/><!-- output UNICODE -->
```

Listing 5.4 Forcing a particular output encoding

One last note: if you are using IE 5 or above, you may choose to run the transform directly in the browser. See the How And Why section in the Basic XSLT topic for more information.

CORE CONCEPTS

Where to Use XSLT

XSLT can be used almost anywhere: on a web server, in an application, or even in a browser. Before we see how to do this, let's recall how CSS is used with XML, then we'll contrast CSS and XSLT.

CSS and XML

We saw in Chapter 4 how CSS can be used to style not just HTML but also XML in an XML-capable browser. It is important to remember that CSS does not translate an XML file into HTML; only XSLT can perform such a transformation. However, an XML file may reference a CSS file, and if a browser is XML/CSS capable, it will, upon navigating to the XML file, make another round trip to the server and request the CSS

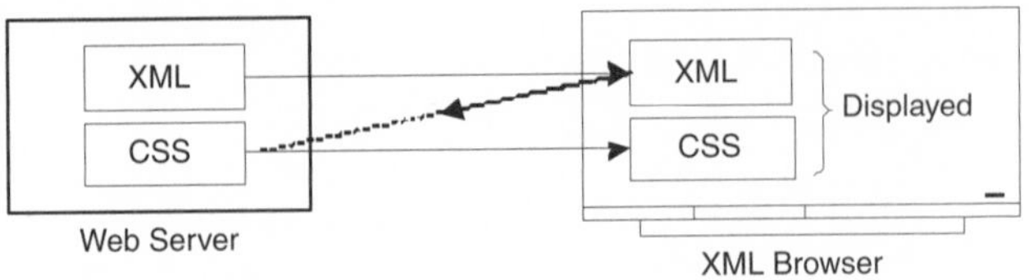

Figure 5.1 Styling XML on the browser using CSS

file referenced by the XML document (see Figure 5.1). The browser will then read styling information from the CSS file and present the XML document much like an HTML document. While fast, simple, and easy, there are many disadvantages to this approach. First, we require an XML-compatible browser. We must also do without JavaScript, HTML forms, Applets, and other rich HTML features that cannot be contained in an XML file or a CSS file. Additionally, the structure of the XML file must be similar to what is required on-screen.

XSLT on the Web Server

XSLT offers an alternative to CSS by *transforming* the XML into HTML instead of simply styling it. Typically a web server is configured (or programmed) to perform this translation. For example, imagine that a client requests some form of report from a website that, behind the scenes, is created from a database query. The database query results in an XML file. The web server then transforms the XML file to an HTML page via an XSLT file located on the server.

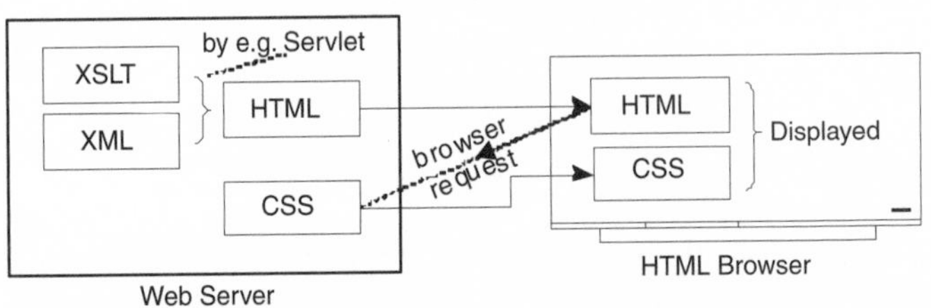

Figure 5.2 Styling XML on the server using XSLT, and then styling the resulting HTML on the browser using CSS

Using this approach, we can target almost any browser, since the browser will be given only the final HTML page and will never see or know about the original XML file. CSS, in the scenario above, is relegated to its usual role, which is styling the HTML. You might, of course, embed the CSS styling information in XSLT so it is *in situ* with the HTML, but typically separate CSS files are used in order to centralize styling aspects (background color and pattern, standard naviagation bar, etc.) that are the same for all the web pages of your site.

To actually perform the transformation from XML to HTML, we require a Servlet or some other traditional web server technology.

XSLT on Any Server

XSLT does not have to be used to generate HTML. In fact, XSLT does not have to be related to the Internet technologies at all. You might use XSLT strictly as a server-side processing engine, to convert between one XML grammar and another as a way of processing data.

XSLT on the Browser

If you are targeting an XSLT-compatible browser, you can move the transform to the client. The advantage of this scenario is that you do not need any server-side code; the browser will do all the processing for you. As was the case with CSS/XML, this frees the web server, allowing it to be concerned only with generating XML:

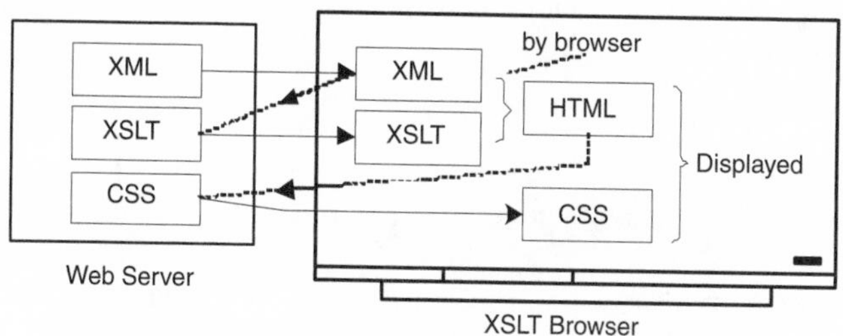

Figure 5.3 Styling XML on the browser using XSLT, and the resulting HTML using CSS

In Figure 5.3, the XSLT browser navigates to an XML file with a stylesheet-processing instruction. Only this time, the instruction references an XSLT stylesheet instead of a CSS stylesheet. The XSLT file will then be retrieved by the browser and the transform applied. The XSLT file, in turn, may add a reference to a CSS file in the HTML page it creates. Thus, the dynamically generated HTML is displayed, with the help of the CSS stylesheet to which it refers.

How XSLT Works

Matching Rules

At the most fundamental level, XSLT processors operate by matching rules, called templates, against a source XML. When matched, these templates create fragments of output, usually based on values from the XML input document. In Listing 5.2, for example, our template generated HTML `<HTML>`, `<BODY>`, and `<H1>` elements, along with the message text (the data between the `<message>` and `</message>` elements) from the source document. To retrieve the message, we used the XSLT instruction `xsl:value-of`, which finds values based on an XPath query (explained later in this chapter).

Templates use the `xsl:apply-templates` instruction to request that additional parts of the input XML be transformed. This fires more templates, which may generate more output and fire more templates, and so on. This cascade of activity is the basic mechanism by which XSLT generates output given an input document.

Most XSLT files contain a template matching the *root* of the source tree, which is fired automatically to "start things off." This was the case in Listing 5.2:

```
<xsl:template match="/">
```

The above line creates a template matching the root element of the source XML.

An XSLT stylesheet is therefore nothing more than a list of rules, usually accompanied by a few top-level instructions for general issues such as what type of character encodings the document should use. Here is a schematic of an XSLT file:

```
<?xml version="1.0"?>
<xsl:stylesheet
  version="1.0"
  xmlns:xsl="http://www.w3.org/1999/XSL/Transform">

top-level instructions (such as encoding of output data)

  <xsl:template match="first match condition">
    instructions for first rule
  </xsl:template>

  <xsl:template match="second match condition">
```

```
    instructions for second rule
  </xsl:template>
  ...
</xsl:stylesheet>
```

Listing 5.5 Schematic layout of an XSLT file

XPath in XSLT

The XPath query language is used throughout XSLT. In Listing 5.2, the value of the `xsl:template match` attribute, which starts the processing chain at the root of the XML document:

```
<xsl:template match="/">
```

and of the `xsl:value-of select` attribute, which actually extracted the character data between the `<text>` and `</text>` tags:

```
<xsl:value-of select="./message/text()"/>
```

are both XPath expressions. These expressions are called *location paths,* and they point to specific locations in the XML in much the same way that a file path points to a particular location in a disk drive's directory system. `text()` is the XPath *function* used to specify the text contained within the `<message>` element.

In addition to specifying paths, XPath can be used during the transformation process to manipulate strings, perform numerical calculations, and so on.

Namespaces

XSLT makes tangential use of XML namespaces. Namespaces are discussed in Chapter 3 (XML Essentials). If, however, you are eager to get started with XSLT, you don't need to give a lot of thought to how namespaces actually operate; just know that you *must* prefix XSLT instructions with "`xsl:`". Any template element without this prefix will simply be written to the destination document rather than executed.

Additionally, be sure the `xsl:stylesheet` line of your XSLT file reads exactly as follows:

```
<xsl:stylesheet
  version="1.0"
  xmlns:xsl="http://www.w3.org/1999/XSL/Transform">
```

Be particularly careful typing the (case-sensitive) URI—the `http://www.w3.org/1999/XSL/Transform` namespace identifies the document as XSLT.

Note that the `xsl` prefix is just a convention; in reality, you can use any prefix to qualify XSLT instructions, as long as you associate it with the correct XSLT namespace.

Topic: Basic XSLT

This topic introduces the fundamentals of XSLT: how to write templates, and how they work together to create output. The topics that follow this one essentially cover the many details of this process—sorting output, formatting, etc.

XSLT instructions are identified using the `xsl` prefix. (Again, this is a convention, not a rule — but we'll follow the convention in this chapter.) If you are familiar with ASP or JSP, you can think of the `xsl` prefix as being similar to the <% and %> delimiters that identify source code of an otherwise ordinary HTML document. An element in the stylesheet not tagged with `xsl` is considered an output element. For example, referring back to Listing 5.2, the `html` element was an output element, not an XSLT command.

A suggestion: While XSLT is not source code in the usual sense, there can be considerable logic encoded within stylesheets. You will find them much easier to work with when they are readable and correctly indented.

CONCEPTS

Applying Templates

Outputting a List

Suppose you had a list of messages in an XML document, and you wanted to write them out as an HTML numbered list. Let's assume the messages are presented as follows:

```
<?xml version="1.0"?>
<system>
  <stamp>12-03-02 23:13</stamp>
  <msgs>
    <msg type="info">System started</msg>
```

```
    <msg type="info">Logging in user 'maryk'</msg>
    <msg type="warn">User 'bobm' not found</msg>
  </msgs>
  . . .
</system>
```

Listing 5.6 System messages for display

Recall that the root element can be matched automatically by the processor. Let's use this rule as a starting point:

```
<xsl:template match="/system">
  <html><body style="font:normal larger tahoma">
  <h3>Log started: <xsl:value-of select="./stamp/text()"/></h3>
  <ol>
    <xsl:apply-templates select="./msgs/msg"/>
  </ol>
  </body></html>
</xsl:template>
```

Listing 5.7 Rule for outputting all messages as an ordered list

Above we selected the `<system>` element as the base element for this template. We outputted the contents of the `<stamp>` element using the `xsl:value-of` command. We then used `xsl:apply-templates` within an `<ol>` element. Recall that `xsl:apply-templates` kicks off the transformation template responsible for the nodes matching the `select` attribute (in this case, all `<msg>` elements). Thus, in the case of Listing 5.7, the line:

```
<xsl:apply-templates select="./msgs/msg"/>
```

is saying, in effect, "fire the template that handles the `<msg>` elements that are descendents of `<msgs>`." The corresponding "match" for this select is:

```
<xsl:template match="msg">
  <li><xsl:value-of select="./text()"/></li>
</xsl:template>
```

Listing 5.8 Rule for outputting a message as a list item

The above template is called by the `xsl:apply-templates` in Listing 5.7 every time a `<msg>` element is encountered by the processor.

The two rules defined in Listing 5.7 and 5.8 combine to produce a proper XSL file. If you take this XSL file and create the corresponding XML file shown in Listing 5.6, you can implement the XML-to-HTML transformation yourself using the processor of your choice (SAXON, etc.).

The final output appears as follows:

```
<html><body>
  <h2>Log started: 12-03-02 23:13</h2>
  <ol>
    <li>System started</li>
    <li>Logging in user 'maryk'</li>
    <li>User 'bobm' not found</li>
  </ol>
</body></html>
```

Listing 5.9 Messages transformed to an HTML list (indentation added for clarity)

If the contents of Listing 5.9 are redirected into an HTML file, a browser will display this new file as:

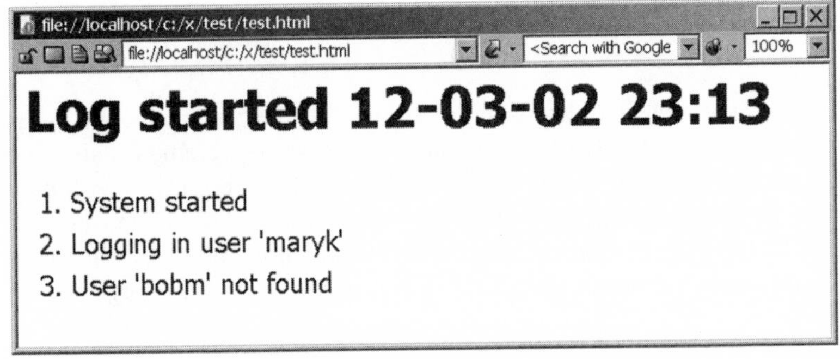

Figure 5.4 An XML log file rendered using XSLT

To recap, we were presented with an XML document that we wished to render in a browser. To accomplish this task, we avoided any programming and instead used XSLT to create a transformation stylesheet. When our XML file is passed through our XSL file, the `<msg>` elements in the source XML are mapped or translated into HTML tags. These HTML tags are output to a file, and we end up with a new HTML document.

Context

One way to think about XSLT files is as a chain of rules that fire each other. To further demonstrate this and to introduce the important concept of *context,* Listings 5.7 and 5.8 are brought together in Listing 5.10

below. Note that we have added line numbers purely for the purpose of example; line numbers are, of course, not part of XSL.

```
1: <xsl:template match="/system">
2:    <html><body style="font:normal larger tahoma">
3:    <h3>Log started: <xsl:value-of
          select="./stamp/text()"/></h3>
4:    <ol>
5:      <xsl:apply-templates select="./msgs/msg"/>
6:    </ol>
7:    </body></html>
8: </xsl:template>
9: <xsl:template match="msg">
10:   <li><xsl:value-of select="./text()"/></li>
11:</xsl:template>
```

Listing 5.10 Messages transformed to an HTML list (indentation added for clarity)

You may recall that this chain of templates must kick off with some element, usually the root. In this case, we can use either match="/system" or match="/"; either syntax is correct. Returning now to contexts: navigating with a context in XSLT is very much like navigating through a file system on a hard drive with a current directory. As a result of line 1, you can think of yourself as "in" the <system> directory. In line 3, "./stamp/text()" indicates that we are interested in the data stored in the <stamp> element, which also resides in <system>. The '.' has the same meaning for XSLT as it does for file systems; that is, *relative* from my current context. <stamp> can be said to be in or "below" <system>, so "./stamp" is the appropriate way to reference the <stamp> element.

The statement on line 5 is saying, "relative to where I am now, there is a <msgs> element, and within that element, there exist one or many <msg> elements. Find a template that knows how to handle <msg> elements, and fire it." We then jump to line 9, where a template that knows how to transform <msg> elements exists. Returning to our file analogy, we can now think of ourselves as in the directory system/msgs where there exist <msg> elements. The template that is now in charge will fire once for each <msg> element that exists. Line 10 states that each time the template fires, the textual data contained by the current <msg> element is to be retrieved and placed between the HTML <li> tags.

Now that we understand how contexts change as we move through an XSL document, we can think of context as simply the node in the XML input file currently under consideration by an instruction in a template.

Accessing Attributes

Suppose you were working on a template to process inventory records having the following form in XML:

```
<item id="31741" q="12">tshirt</item>
<item id="31752" q="19">banner</item>
```

You would like to output these records as HTML, specifically as follows:

```
<div>31741 (tshirt): 12</div>
<div>31752 (banner): 19</div>
```

Clearly, we need to extract both the values of attributes *and* the text data stored by the source element. Fortunately, this is simple to do. Attributes are accessed using the "@" character, as shown in the example below:

```
<xsl:template match="item">
  <div>
    <xsl:value-of select="@id "/>
    (<xsl:value-of select="./text()"/>):
    <xsl:value-of select="@q"/>
  </div>
</xsl:template>
```

Listing 5.11 Accessing attributes

Listing 5.11 outputs the value of the `id` attribute, followed by the text contents of the `<item>` element, followed by the value of the `q` attribute.

We can, in fact, simplify this template using *string concatenation.* The three lines in boldface in Listing 5.11 are equivalent to:

```
<xsl:value-of select="concat(@id,' (',text(),'): ',@q)"/>
```

We'll examine `concat()` and other string manipulation functions later in this chapter.

Wildcards

Elements

The wildcard character "*" is used when you wish to match against any element. For example, suppose you are processing a list of employees structured in XML as follows:

```
<employees>
  <manager><name>Jennifer Lo</name></manager>
  <vp><name>Caldera Peng</name></vp>
  <developer><name>Familia Muesli</name></developer>
  . . .
</employees>
```

In this XML file, the `<name>` element occurs in many different places and, possibly, at different nesting levels. It may be that you want a single template to handle all employee names in an identical fashion. This is easy to do, as a wildcard is all that is necessary. You can match the contents of `<name>` elements for *all* employees using:

```
<xsl:apply-templates select="/employees/*/name"/>
```

The wildcard can also be used in conjunction with aggregate functions (discussed later in this chapter) such as `count ()`. To determine the total number of employees, you could use this command:

```
<xsl:apply-templates select="count(/employees/*)/>
```

We'll examine `count()` and other aggregate functions in the upcoming topic.

Note that `/employees/*` represents a set of nodes, or *nodeset.* If, instead of applying templates, you tried to output the value of a nodeset using `xsl:value-of` (essentially, casting the nodeset to a string), you would see only the text of the first element.

Attributes

The wildcard character `"*"` can also be used with attributes, in the form `"@*"`. For example:

```
<xsl:apply-templates select="./@*"/>
```

This example would apply templates to any and all attributes of the current node. We haven't seen a template that matches on attributes yet, which brings us to the question of what happens in such a situation. To answer that question, we'll need to examine default templates.

Default Templates

What happens when `xsl:apply-templates` is invoked but no matching template exists? Will XSLT throw an exception? Will the transformation fail? Thankfully neither—as a last resort, a default set of templates is built in to XSLT to handle any unmatched nodes. Don't expect too much from the default templates, however. They will simply take all values from the unmatched nodes and pass them through as output. Here is the implicit default rule for unmatched elements:

```
<xsl:template match="*|/">
  <xsl:apply-templates select="*"/>
</xsl:template>
```

The | sign is read as "union," and functions like a logical OR. In other words, the above built-in template matches any child elements (*) as well as the root element (/). The template itself calls `xsl:apply-templates` for all its children.

The default template for attributes is shown here:

```
<xsl:template match="text()|@*">
  <xsl:value-of select="."/>
</xsl:template>
```

In other words, if unmatched by the explicit rules, the value of a text node or attribute node will be output.

Accessing Parent Elements with ".."

In many file systems, the characters ".." are used to reference a directory one level above the current. In XSLT this syntax is used to reference a node that is one level up, e.g., the parent of the current context node.

Consider, for example, an input document that pairs new employees of various divisions with mentors:

```
<mentors>
  <mentor>sallym<sales>dougn</sales></mentor>
  <mentor>samp<ops>peters</ops></mentor>
  <mentor>bobg<sales>jillp</sales></mentor>
  <!--  . . .  -->
</mentors>
```

Listing 5.12 New employees and their mentors

How might we output a list that includes *only* the new sales employees and their mentors? While there are many possible approaches, in the following example, we'll first locate all the sales employees, and from each access his or her manager using "..":

```
<xsl:template match="/">
  <xsl:apply-templates select="mentors/mentor/sales"/>
</xsl:template>

<xsl:template match="sales">
  <div><xsl:value-of select="./text()"/>'s mentor is
  <xsl:value-of select="../text()"/></div>
</xsl:template>
```

Listing 5.13 Extracting sales employees and their mentors

Notice that we use `"../text()"` to access the name of the salesperson. If we had just used "..", this line would have resulted in the mentor and the salesperson being output, instead of just the mentor.

The XSLT stylesheet in Listing 5.13, applied to the XML in Listing 5.12, produces the following list of salespeople and their mentors:

```
dougn's mentor is sallym
jillp's mentor is bobg
```

Recursive Descent

The special recursive descent operator `//` can be used to find all nodes of a particular type, regardless of their location. Consider, for example, a large XML document that contains many different products and their prices. If you want to apply some action to all price elements no matter where they might be scattered in the document, you can apply templates to one of the following:

Pattern	Action
`<xsl:apply-templates select="//"/>`	act on all notation nodes in the document
`<xsl:apply-templates select=".//"/>`	act on all notation descendents of the current context node

Table 5.1 Relative and absolute recursive descent

You will only occasionally need `//`. It is simply an easy technique for finding all nodes of a particular type.

EXAMPLE

For the example that follows, assume we have the XML file shown in Listing 5.14, which contains the XML description of a small construction job:

```
<?xml version="1.0"?>
<job name="install signpost">
  <contractors>
    <contractor id="1">Jumbo Supplies</contractor>
    <contractor id="2">Thompson Fixtures</contractor>
    <contractor id="3">Bob's Hardware</contractor>
  </contractors>

  <specifics>
    <tools contractor_id ="3">
      <tool count="1">shovel</tool>
      <tool count="4">clamps</tool>
    </tools>

    <materials contractor_id ="1">
      <material amount="2 x 50lb">bag of cement</material>
      <material amount="15">screws</material>
      <material amount="2 x 1l">outdoor sealer</material>
    </materials>
  </specifics>
</job>
```

Listing 5.14 Construction job sample XML data

Note that the examples that follow are written for clarity and are somewhat abbreviated—the files generated by our transformations are not complete HTML documents, though they will nonetheless display in most any browser.

Displaying a List of All Contractors

Listing 5.15 defines a rule to match any contractor:

```
<xsl:template match="contractor">
  <div><xsl:value-of select="@id"/>.
  <xsl:value-of select="text()"/></div>
</xsl:template>
```

```
<!--BELOW: Override default behaviour of text()-->
<xsl:template match="text()"/>
```

Listing 5.15 XSLT to extract contractors from XML in Listing 5.14

The last line of Listing 5.15 may require a refresher to understand; its purpose is subtle. Remember that the implicit default rules of XSLT (see the previous section, "Default Templates") dictate that if an element does *not* have a corresponding matching template, its text and the text of its children will automatically be output by XSL's default `text()` function (assuming, of course, that templates do not exist for the children). If, however, a template exists for a given element, neither that element nor its children will be automatically output; it will be up to the template to perform this output for the element and its children. The final line of Listing 5.15 overrides the default behavior of `text()` such that it will no longer output *any* element or data that does not have a template.

Since there exists only one template matching the contractor, and this template outputs the `@id` attribute, only contractor information will ultimately be output.

When the XML of Listing 5.14 is transformed via the XSLT of Listing 5.15, we will have:

```
1. Jumbo Supplies
2. Thompson Fixtures
3. Bob's Hardware
```

Listing 5.16 Output from XSLT in Listing 5.15 applied to XML in Listing 5.13

Displaying a List of Job Specifics

Listing 5.17 below demonstrates the matching of any grandchild of the `specifics` element. Specifically, we are trying to determine the type and count of tools/materials each contractor is using, and the amount of each :

```
<xsl:template match="/job/specifics/*/*">
  <div>
    contractor
    <xsl:value-of select="../@contractor_id"/>:
    <xsl:value-of select="text()"/>
    (<xsl:value-of select="@count"/>
    <xsl:value-of select="@amount"/>)
```

```
  </div>
</xsl:template>

<xsl:template match="text()"/>
```

Listing 5.17 XSLT to extract job details from XML in Listing 5.14

In order to output the @count- or @amount, we retrieve both attributes for every child of specifics. However, since <tools> has a count attribute, and <materials> has an amount, one of the two attributes will always be an empty string. We'll see in an upcoming section how to use conditional expressions to avoid printing the empty string, but for now we will work around it. Our output will be:

```
contractor 3: shovel (1)
contractor 3: clamps (4)
contractor 1: bag of cement (2 x 50lb)
contractor 1: screws (15)
contractor 1: outdoor sealer (2 x 1l)
```

Listing 5.18 Output from XSLT in Listing 5.17 applied to XML in Listing 5.14

HOW AND WHY

Is the URL in xsl:stylesheet Actually Used?

No. The second line of your XSLT file *declares* itself as XSLT with:

```
<xsl:stylesheet
  version="1.0"
  xmlns:xsl="http://www.w3.org/1999/XSL/Transform">
```

The URI here is just a key, a unique value, also known as a namespace. URLs are frequently used as namespaces simply because they are a convenient set of globally unique values. See "Namespaces" in Chapter 3 of this CodeNote for details on namespace URIs.

If you wish, of course, you can follow the URL in a browser to verify there is little of interest at this location.

How Do I Use XSLT 1.0 in My Browser?

The mechanics of this approach are identical to using CSS to style XML on a browser, as outlined in Chapter 4 (Styling with CSS).

First the browser is directed at an XML document, which references an (XSLT) stylesheet using a processing instruction. For example:

```
<?xml version="1.0"?>
<?xml-stylesheet type="text/xsl" href="render.xsl"?>
. . .
```

Listing 5.19 Rendering XML using XSLT on a browser

As of this writing, IE 6.0 is the only browser that natively supports XSLT 1.0, but see also XSLT Support in IE 5.x under Bugs and Caveats below.

For alternate approaches to browser-side XSLT transforms, see CodeNotes Pointer CN XM000107, "XML Programming with JavaScript."

Note that the value for the "type" `attribute` in Listing 5.19, "`text/xsl`", will work with IE 6.0 and above. Varying standards specify slightly different values, e.g., "`text/xml`" and "`text/xml-xsl`"; it is unclear at the time of this writing which value will be adopted by future browsers.

How Do I Use XSLT 1.0 on My Web Server?

XSLT can be a very useful tool for generating dynamic web content, but can be used in isolation only in simple cases. You will likely need to combine XSLT with other technologies. A few examples using Servlets:

- The Servlet may *transform the XSLT itself.* Consider a form that requests a sort order—the Servlet might handle submission of this form by modifying an XSLT `xsl:sort` tag using the DOM, and then applying the XSLT to return the sorted table as requested.
- XSLT might be used for *fragments of a page,* or a subset of the frames. Potentially tricky or code-intensive functionality such as personalized frame layouts might more easily be done using Servlets.
- A Servlet might *post-process* the output of an XSLT transform to add formatting to fields that could not be added using XSLT.

Whichever decision makes sense for you, a central requirement is performing a transform under the control of a web server. Below are examples in JSP and ASP:

JSP

In this example we perform a transform using the Apache tag library:

```
<%@taglib prefix="x"
    uri="http://jakarta.apache.org/taglibs/xsl/1.0"%>
<x:apply xml="data.xml" xsl="render.xsl"/>
```

Listing 5.20 JSP generating output with XSLT

For full details on installing and using Servlets, JSP, and other Java web technologies, see *CodeNotes for J2EE.*

ASP

In this example we load XML and XSLT from disk, and use the Microsoft DOM extension function `transformNode()` to apply the XSLT to the XML. The resulting string is written directly to the response stream.

```
<%@ LANGUAGE="VBScript" %>
<%
  Set data = Server.CreateObject("MSXML2.DOMDocument")
  data.async = False
  data.load Server.MapPath("data.xml")

  Set render = Server.CreateObject("MSXML2.DOMDocument")
  render.async = False
  render.load Server.MapPath("render.xsl")

  Response.Write data.transformNode(render)
%>
```

Listing 5.21 ASP generating output with XSLT

ASP is available as part of the Internet Information Services (IIS) package that comes preinstalled on Windows 2000 and later operating systems. MSXML 3 has a number of features specific to server-side processing, including free-threaded DOM objects and precompiled XSLT stylesheets.

Can I Use DOM or SAX Instead of XSLT?

Yes. Any transform that can be written using XSLT could theoretically also be written using a traditional programming language and either the DOM or SAX API (see Chapters 6 and 7 for more information). However, it would generally take much longer to develop. Unless you have extremely large XML input files or require an extremely optimized transform, you should consider transforming XML using XSLT before either DOM or SAX.

BUGS AND CAVEATS

XSLT Support in IE 5.x

IE 5.x, by default, supports an obsolete draft standard of XSLT, bearing the confusing name of XSL (XSL now refers to a family of standards, of which XSLT is a member). Under particular circumstances, taking advantage of this draft support may be used to good effect. See the CodeNotes website CN XM000588 for mechanics, as well as pros and cons, of this approach.

You can actually see an example of the draft support if you have IE 5.x. The collapsable tree IE uses to display XML files without CSS or XSLT processing directives is, in fact, the result of an XSL transform—the source can be seen using the URL:

```
res://msxml.dll/defaultss.xsl
```

Notice in particular the namespace:

```
http://www.w3.org/TR/WD-xsl
```

`WD`, of course, stands for Working Draft.

A much better approach, however, is to upgrade IE 5.x to full XSLT 1.0 support by installing MSXML 3 in "Replace Mode." See Chapter 2 (Installation) for more information on installing MSXML 3.

Avoid //

The recursive descent operator `//` involves visiting every node of the input XML. This is an expensive operation that should be avoided where possible. Use regular location paths instead.

SUMMARY

XPath is used extensively in XSLT to select nodes. A template's context determines the location in the XML input from which XPath locations are based, in order to extract values using `xsl:value-of`, apply additional templates using `xsl:apply-templates`, etc. When `xsl:apply-templates` is used, an XSLT template is "fired" or, if none matches, then the default template rules are used.

In this topic we've examined the fundamental workings of XSLT. Understanding how a set of templates generates output and learning how to navigate an input XML using XPath is as difficult as XSLT gets. With the grounding provided by this topic, we can now examine XPath types and functions in order to begin formatting and refining output.

Topic: Formatting with XPath

Consider an XSLT stylesheet that builds an HTML sales report. We would ideally like to format our numeric values (e.g., `$1,498.43`) and manipulate strings (e.g., output a date in mm/dd/yy format when given yy/mm/dd).

XPath contains just enough typing and manipulation capabilities to perform these tasks easily. XPath supports numbers, booleans, strings, and nodesets (a group of nodes, often returned as a result of using a wildcard), and has a small library of functions for working with each. XSLT 1.0 does *not,* however, support powerful manipulation capabilities, such as regular expressions, or a built-in general purpose scripting language. See the Bugs and Caveats entry Intensive Type Manipulation, below, for more details on the options available.

In this topic we'll cover string and number support, which are used in the Controlling Output topic that follows this one. XPath booleans are covered in the Sorting and Filtering topic, where they are of greater importance.

CONCEPTS

Working with Strings

Functions

The XSLT string library is simple enough to illustrate by way of example. Let's work from the context of the `name` element below:

```
<name id="WA3156">
  <first>Bob</first>
  <last>Smith</last>
  <born>25/05/1972</born>
</name>
```

Listing 5.22 Sample data for Table 5.2 string operations

Demonstrated in Table 5.2 are the most commonly used functions. Each example is carefully chosen to illustrate a particular functionality:

Operation	**<xsl:value-of select=____/>**	**result**
string length	**"string-length(@id)"**	6
adding strings	**"concat(first, last)"** **"concat(first, ' ', last)** **"concat('id:', @id)"**	Bob Smith Bob Smith id:WA3156
extracting	**"substring(born, 7) "**	1972
substrings	**"substring(born, 14, 2)"** **"substring-before(born, '/')"**	05 25
comparisons	**"contains(born, '1972')"** **"starts-with(@id, 'PA')"** **" 'Bob' = 'bob' "** **" 'Smith' = last"**	true false false true

Table 5.2 String operations

From the examples in Table 5.2 it should be clear that `substring()` is 1-based (not 0-based), that the operators = and `!=` are case-sensitive, and that `concat()` accepts two or more arguments.

Literals

When working with string literals in XPath, we will often need to use entity references to represent certain characters (quotes in particular). The following table demonstrates how the attribute quotes and string literals interact:

<xsl:value-of select=___/>	**returns**
" 'abc' " **' "abc" '** **' "What's up?" '** **" '"howdy"' "** **" 'out & aboot' "**	abc abc What's up? "howdy" out & aboot

Table 5.3 Expressing literals in XPath

Working with Numbers

XPath supports a single high-precision floating-point numerical type. You may convert an expression *`expr`* to a number using `number(expr)`. If *`expr`* does not represent a number, the result is the string `NaN` (Not A Number). This (error) condition can be detected using `string(number(expr))='NaN'`. For example:

```
<xsl:if test="string(number(@id))='NaN'">
  Error, id is not numeric!
</xsl:if>
```

The above example prints an error message if `@id` does not represent a number—we'll examine `xsl:if` in the Sorting and Filtering topic later in this chapter.

Basic Arithmetic

XPath supports the following numeric operators: `+`, `-`, `*`, `div`, and `mod`.

There should be nothing surprising here except for `div`. To divide `v1` by `v2` use `v1 div v2` instead of `v1 / v2`. This is necessary as XML reserves the use of `/`. `mod` stands for *modulus,* the remainder of a division. For example,

```
<xsl:value-of select="8 mod 3"/>
```

evaluates to `2`.

Aggregate Functions

Two simple aggregate functions are available to total up values:

- `sum(`*`nodeset`*`)` totals the numeric values of specified nodes.
- `count(`*`nodeset`*`)` counts the number of nodes.

For example, to output the average price of all the stocks in a list like this one:

```
<stock symbol="YAF" price="134.9052"/>
<bond symbol="GOV7" price="87.5635"/>
<stock symbol="OIU" price="17.1095"/>
<!--  . . .  -->
```

you might, from the context of the parent node, use:

```
<xsl:value-of select="sum(stock/@price) div count(stock)"/>
```

Note that `"sum(stock/@price)"` in the example above is not stock divided by `@price`. Rather, it is the `@price` attribute of a `stock` element.

Rounding Numbers

XSLT also supports rounding:

- `ceiling(expr)` rounds up
- `floor(expr)` rounds down
- `round(expr)` rounds to the nearest integer

For example, one way to output a `@price` attribute, rounded to two digits, is:

```
<xsl:value-of select="round(@price * 100) / 100"/>
```

Element Indices

Two XPath functions return information about the current context:

- `position()` returns the 1-based sibling number of the context node.
- `last()` returns the number of children of the parent of the context node.

For example, you might use `<xsl:value-of select="position()"/>` to number a list of items (though `xsl:number` is an alternative CN XM000510. These methods will become especially useful when we examine conditionals later in the chapter.

Depending on the XSLT parser you are using, whitespace may be counted as a sibling node instead of being ignored. You can fix this problem by using a DTD to define the XML document or by removing the whitespace from the XML file.

Formatting Numbers

The `format-number()` function formats a number according to a formatting string. An example of such a string is `"#.00"`, which would ensure that at least two decimal places were always visible. This format is similar to that accepted by Java's `java.text.DecimalFormat` and VB's `Format()`.

You may differentiate formatting for positive and negative values by separating two patterns with a semicolon (`";"`). For negative patterns, `"#"` is used as a placeholder for the numeric value. The examples below in Table 5.4 have been chosen to illustrate the various aspects of `xsl:format-number`:

Pattern	Values	Result
$#,##0.00;($#)	15993.5 −.587	$15,993.50 ($0.59)
00.0%	.857	85.7%
00.0% (up);#% (down)	−1.4	140.0% (down)

Table 5.4 Formatting numbers

`format-number()` provides additional formatting control to change the grouping separator (`","` by default), use named formats, and so on. See the CodeNotes website `XM000511` for more details and examples.

Note that `format-number()` is available only when XPath is used in conjunction with XSLT.

Using Variables

XSLT can be said to support variables, although this may be an unfortunate choice of terminology; XSLT variables are really more like constants. For example, consider the following XSLT statements:

```
<xsl:value-of select="/dy/usr/ny/cr/info/firstName"/>
<xsl:value-of select="/dy/usr/ny/cr/info/lastName"/>
```

This code can be made more maintainable (and efficient, if the common subexpression is complex) by creating a variable named `$details` to hold the shared parent node `info`:

```
<xsl:variable name="details" select="/dy/usr/ny/cr/info"/>

<xsl:value-of select="$details/firstName"/>
<xsl:value-of select="$details/lastName"/>
```

Listing 5.23 Using variables to factor out a common location path

Notice the `details` variable is declared and initialized at the same time, and is always dereferenced with a `$`.

Variables in XSLT are *scoped,* which means they are visible only within the context in which they were created. If declared with *global* scope (i.e., as a top-level element), a variable is visible to every rule of the stylesheet.

EXAMPLE

Assume we are presented with the following XML representing inventory data:

```
<?xml version="1.0"?>
<inventory>
  <item name="redones" num="2"/>
  <item name="blueones" num="1"/>
  <item name="orangeones" num="2"/>
</inventory>
```

Listing 5.24 Inventory of a bag of candy

We wish to generate a simple HTML report, as shown below:

```
1. redones (2)
2. blueones (1)
3. orangeones (2)
---------------
total pieces: 5
```

Listing 5.25 Contents of a workshop—output

To generate the report of 5.25, we can make use of several of the functions presented in this topic, including `position()` to number the list and `sum()` to calculate the total number of pieces. We will also introduce the `xsl:if` statement (covered in greater detail in the Sorting and Filtering topic, below).

```
<xsl:template match="item">
  <div>
    <xsl:value-of select="position()"/>.
    <xsl:value-of select="@name"/>
    (<xsl:value-of select="@num"/>)
  </div>

  <xsl:if test="position()=last()">
    <div>---------------</div>
    <div>total pieces:
      <xsl:value-of select="sum(../item/@num)"/>
    </div>
  </xsl:if>
</xsl:template>
```

Listing 5.26 Contents of a workshop—transform

Remember, depending on the XSLT processor you are using, you may have to remove the whitespace in Listing 5.24 for the transformation to work properly.

HOW AND WHY

Changing Case

XSL has no built-in case conversion function. There is good reason for this—XML supports many different character encodings, and determining the required character conversions can be difficult and context-specific.

If, however, you are working solely with the English alphabet, then you can patch together a solution using the `translate()` function. The expression below converts the value of `StockSymbol` to uppercase:

```
<xsl:value-of select="translate(StockSymbol,
  'abcdefghijklmnopqrstuvwxyz',
  'ABCDEFGHIJKLMNOPQRSTUVWXYZ')"/>
```

Listing 5.27 Conversion to uppercase (English alphabet only)

In the upcoming Working with Templates topic we'll see how to store this logic in a *named template* (like a function in a program) so we can reuse it without copying.

BUGS AND CAVEATS

Expressing Single and Double Quotes in One Literal String

Strings such as `"who's that!"` cannot be expressed as XPath literals, though there are at least two workarounds.

One option is using `concat()` on strings using entities. The following expression has the value `'"'`:

```
concat('&quot;',&quot;&apos;&quot;,'&quot;')
```

An alternative is to use variables, as in:

```
<xsl:variable name="apos" select="'"/>
<xsl:variable name="quot" select='"'/>
```

The string `'"'` can now be expressed as `$apos;$quot;$apos;`.

Intensive Type Manipulation

While it is possible to perform intensive analytics (e.g., curve fitting) or complex string manipulation on XML input using XPath, it is often not maintainable, efficient, or advisable.

For these situations you may consider pre- or postprocessing your data using a programming language combined with either DOM (Chapter 6) or SAX (Chapter 7). Another option is to take advantage of whatever general programming support your XSLT processor offers, as described below.

General Programming Support for XSLT

When faced with difficult processing tasks, the convenience of being able to access Java or a scripting language from XSLT is undeniable. Unfortunately XSLT 1.0 does not specify a standard mechanism to access outside languages.

The popular XSLT processors, discussed in Chapter 2 (Installation) do, however, provide *proprietary* extension mechanisms. The Xalan processor built into JAXP, for example, permits access to Java, while MSXML supports embedded JScript. For examples of the JAXP and MSXML extension mechanisms, see the CodeNotes website CN XM000503.

Be Sure to Quote Literals with XPath

A common, subtle mistake is forgetting to quote literals when using XPath:

```
<xsl:variable name="egg"
             select="@edu=college or @edu=university"/>
```

Here the strings "college" and "university" should be wrapped with single quotes, otherwise they will be taken as node names. To fix this problem, use:

```
<xsl:variable name="egg"
      select="@edu='college' or @edu='university'"/>
```

SUMMARY

XPath supports manipulating values from the XML input document as strings or numbers, and includes fairly powerful support such as controlling the number of decimal places used when outputting numbers.

XSLT variables can be used to simplify and streamline complex expressions.

If you have considerable processing requirements, such as analytics or parsing free-form text, you should consider leveraging programming language that can access the DOM or SAX APIs.

Topic: Controlling Output

In this topic we'll see how to apply the XPath formatting discussed in the last topic to element and attribute values. We'll also see how to target XML, HTML, or text using `xsl:output`, and we'll discuss a sometimes convenient alternative to rule-based processing using the `xsl:for-each` instruction.

CONCEPTS

Dynamically Valued Attributes

Normally, when mapping an XML file to an HTML file via XSLT, you include the HTML attributes directly in the XSL file. Remember that anything in an XSL file not prefixed by `xsl:` simply gets passed through to the output. Thus, if you wanted the HTML body tag to appear in the HTML document resulting from your XSL transform, you would simply type `<body style="background-color:snow; color:navy"/>` in your XSL file.

Hard-coded HTML attributes are generally all that are required. However, suppose you wish for the HTML attribute to have different values depending on the value of some element of the XML file. You can do this with the `xsl:attribute`.

Imagine that you wanted to create an HTML form dynamically consisting solely of text boxes. Suppose you want to retrieve default values for each text box from an XML file.

The HTML required to create a text field and populate it with a default value is:

```
<input type="text" value="somevalue"></input>
```

Rather than hard-code the value attribute as we have just done, we want the value attribute to get its value from some element in an XML file. To perform this feat, we need to make use of `xsl:attribute` in our XSL file. Examine Listing 5.28:

```
<input type="text">
  <xsl:attribute name="value">
    <xsl:value-of select="./valuefromxmlelement"/>
  </xsl:attribute>
</input>
```

Listing 5.28 Creating an attribute with xsl:attribute in an XSL file

Listing 5.28 demonstrates the creation of a dynamic attribute. The first line is the ordinary HTML element, with one ordinary attribute, `type`. The second line informs the XSL processor that the value attribute is dynamic. The third line will give our dynamic attribute (`value`) the value of the text stored from the XML element `valuefromxmlelement`.

Therefore, if the XML file contained the following:

```
<valuefromxmlelement>42<valuefromxmlelement>
```

The XML file translated via the XSL file containing the dynamic attribute shown in Listing 5.28 will produce the following HTML:

```
<input type="text" value="42"></input>
```

Note that `xsl:attribute` overwrites any existing attribute with the same name in the surrounding element, and must always be located directly under the opening tag of the output element for which it is intended.

Creating Attributes with "{ }"

While useful, the `xsl:attribute` syntax we outlined in the previous section is rather clumsy—three lines are a lot of text to create one small attribute. Fortunately, there is an alternative, formally known as *attribute value templates.* The following XSLT is equivalent to the example in Listing 5.28:

```
<input type="text" value="{./valuefromxmlelement}"></input>
```

You can see that this looks almost like the output from Listing 5.28. The value of the template is delimited with `{}`, which is interpreted as an XPath expression and evaluated, just like an argument to `xsl:value-of`.

Attribute value templates may be used only with literal elements (such as `input`) as well as several XSLT instructions, including `xslt:sort`, which we'll examine in the next topic.

Although the bracketed syntax is convenient, the `xsl:attribute` syntax is sometimes necessary. For example, if you want to write an attribute that is dynamic only under certain conditions and fixed for all others, you'll need to combine `xsl:attribute` with `xsl:if` (we will examine `xsl:if` in the Sorting and Filtering topic.)

Looping—An Alternative to Templates

We have seen several instances where we were presented with a *list* of elements in our input XML, such as:

```
<?xml version="1.0""?>
<stocks>
  <stock>CUPA</stock>
  <stock>ACME</stock>
  <!-- etc -->
</stocks>
```

Listing 5.29 A list of stock items

Consider printing the stocks as an HTML list. Using templates we would write the following:

```
<xsl:template match="/stocks">
  <ol>
    <xsl:apply-templates select="stock"/>
  </ol>
</xsl:template>

<xsl:template match="stock">
  <li>
    <xsl:value-of select="."/>
  </li>
</xsl:template>
```

Listing 5.30 Looping with template matching

There is, however, an alternative nontemplate approach. That approach is to leverage the `xsl:for-each` instruction. Using `xsl:for-each`, we can loop over the `stock` elements in place:

```
<xsl:template match="/">
    <ol>
    <xsl:for-each select="stocks/stock">
      <li>
        <xsl:value-of select="."/>
      </li>
```

```
    </xsl:for-each>
  </ol>
</xsl:template>
```

Listing 5.31 Looping with xsl:for-each

Listings 5.30 and 5.31 produce the identical output, and are roughly equivalent in terms of performance. The template approach of 5.30 is, however, more flexible; it allows for easy reuse of its second template.

Output Formats

By default the XSLT processor writes an XML document. However, we can tailor the output as required using the top-level element `xsl:output`. Top-level elements are any elements that appear directly underneath the root `<xsl:stylesheet>` element.

Text

To create text output with a stylesheet, use:

```
<xsl:stylesheet
  version="1.0"
  xmlns:xsl="http://www.w3.org/1999/XSL/Transform">
<xsl:output method="text"/>
```

This is useful for when you wish to simply output a plain text document instead of XML elements. You might choose text output if you wished to build a comma-separated values (CSV) file for import into a legacy database using a database utility such as `bcp`. In this scenario the required *format file* might also be built using XSLT. See the CodeNotes website CN XM000589 for an example.

Recall that an XSLT file must be well-formed XML—to output `<'` as a delimiter, for example, you would have to use the XML `<` entity reference. See the reference card accompanying this CodeNote for a complete list of XML entities.

HTML

You should specify `<xsl:output method="html">` when targeting HTML. Among several very minor changes, the output will be stripped of unneeded and potentially browser-confounding end-tags, such as the closing horizontal rule, `</HR>`.

Note that to write a literal `<HR>` to the output you would still need to encode the closing `</HR>` within the XSLT document. Otherwise, the XSLT would not be well-formed.

EXAMPLE

Let's consider a set of data extracted from the tracking system of a hardware rental store:

```
<?xml version="1.0"?>
<rentals>
  <rental sn="19050532" status="out">Forklift</rental>
  <rental sn="19050958" status="in">Forklift</rental>
  <rental sn="22855223" status="out">Hand Crane</rental>
  <rental sn="32525112" status="out">Power Hammer</rental>
</rentals>
```

Listing 5.32 Sample machine rental data

We would like to construct an attractive HTML table of the current inventory status for our manager, showing the items as a table and color-coding based on their status. The XSLT is shown here:

```
<xsl:template match="/rentals">
  <style>
    body        { background-color:beige }
    td          { font: normal 8pt tahoma; }
    th          { font: bold 8pt tahoma }
    .head       { font: bold 8pt tahoma; color:white;
                  background-color:black }
    table       { border-color:black; border-style:solid;
                  border-width:1; padding:2 15 2 15; }
    .row_out    { background-color:darkkhaki }
    .row_in     { background-color:khaki }
  </style>

  <table cellpadding="0">
    <tr class="head"><th>Serial</th><th>Name</th></tr>
    <xsl:for-each select="rental">
      <tr class="row_{@status}">
        <td style="text-align:right">
          <xsl:value-of select="@sn"/></td>
        <td><xsl:value-of select="."/></td>
      </tr>
    </xsl:for-each>
  </table>
</xsl:template>
```

Listing 5.33 Attractive table for sample data of Listing 5.32

Above we've selected the table row class using the `status` attribute—a neat trick that color-codes our table rows by availability. We've also used `xsl:for-each` to iterate over the rental elements, saving us a few extra lines. The output is fairly attractive, displayed here using Internet Explorer 5.5:

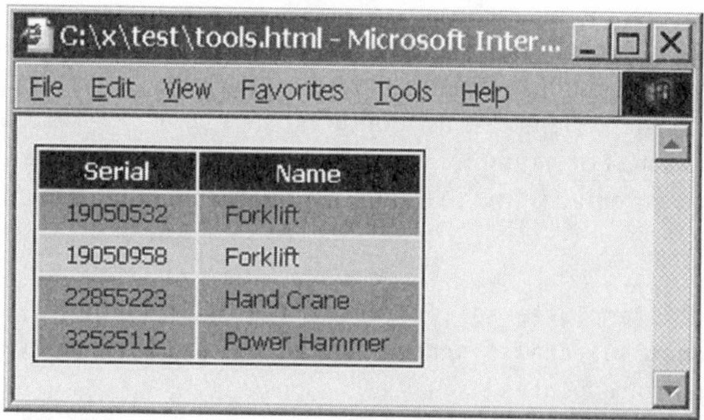

Figure 5.5 Output of Listing 5.33 applied to Listing 5.32

SUMMARY

We have seen several examples in this chapter demonstrating how to enrich our output using both `xsl:attribute` and attribute value templates. We now have the tools we need to target almost any XML grammar. We also investigated `xsl:output-format` for specifically targeting HTML or text documents. Finally, we have seen how `xsl:for-each`, while restricting reuse, can be quicker and easier than using templates to evaluate lists of items.

Topic: Sorting and Filtering

XSLT is undeniably useful for translations. A translation, however, does not always involve changing one type of element to another; sometimes it may involve sorting a large volume of data or filtering that data based on some criteria. Fortunately, both sorting and filtering are easy to perform with XSLT.

Sorting may involve moving high priority items to the front of a list, organizing long lists alphabetically or, perhaps, by id or other attribute. Filtering involves excluding unwanted items from the output and can be accomplished in a few different ways, XPath *predicate-based* node filters, as well as XSLT's more general-purpose `xsl:if` and `xsl:choose`. In this topic, we will discuss both.

CONCEPTS

Sorting Your Output

Sorting a set of output elements is easy using XSLT; simply add one or more `xsl:sort` elements as children of `xsl:apply-templates-` or `xsl:for-each`. For example, to sort a set of `stock` elements based on their text (we will assume that this text represents their ticker symbol), use:

```
<xsl:apply-templates select="stock">
  <xsl:sort select="." order="ascending" data-type="text"/>
</xsl:apply-templates>
```

The `xsl:sort select` attribute tells the processor the sort key—in this case, "."—meaning the current element of our present context. Since we are in a template that handles the `<stock>` element, the `'.'` and the `data-type="text"` attribute identifies that we are sorting the results of the evaluated templates based on a string sort of the data held in <stock> element. We have also stated that our strings are to be sorted in ascending order.

Alternatively, if we wished to sort on the stock price (we will assume that the price exists as an attribute for each stock), from most to least expensive, we can use the following `xsl:sort` instruction:

```
<xsl:sort select="@price"
          order="descending"
          data-type="number"/>
```

The ordering of elements that cannot be converted to a number (i.e., those `NaN` values) is undefined. See the CodeNote reference card for additional sorting options.

Filters

Filters are extremely powerful tools that allow us to exclude data from an XML document that are not of interest (for example, all stocks with a price below some certain threshold). Before examining filters, however, we need to understand XPath booleans, which are expressions whose value is either `true` or `false`.

Working with Booleans

A boolean value results from using any of the following operators:

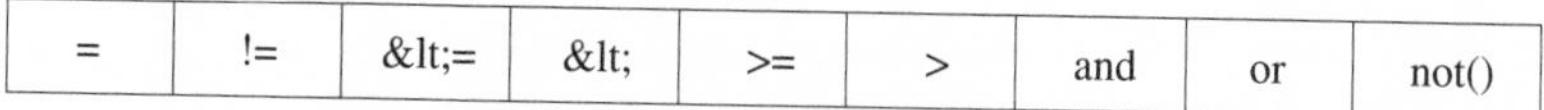

=	!=	<=	<	>=	>	and	or	not()

Table 5.5 XPath boolean operators

By way of demonstration, the following directive will display the string `true` whenever a value `@n` is larger or equal to zero and smaller or equal to 100, and `false` otherwise:

```
<xsl:value-of select="@n >= 0 and @n &lt;= 100"/>
```

Notice that we must express the less than sign (<) using `<` to ensure the XML remains well formed.

You can explicitly create (or *cast*) any expression `expr` to a boolean using `boolean(expr)`. The boolean value an expression becomes depends on the type of expression. For example:

- Casting a string returns true when the string is not the empty string ("").
- Casting a nodeset returns true when there are one or more nodes.
- Casting a number returns true whenever the number is not `0`.

Casting a boolean to a string returns the string `true` or `false` depending, of course, on the value of the boolean.

Filters

To demonstrate the utility and functionality of filters, consider building an HTML page based on the following XML:

```
<msgs>
  <msg error="0" importance="low"> . . . </msg>
  <msg error="0" importance="high"> . . . </msg>
  <msg error="1" importance="low"> . . . </msg>
  <!-- . . . -->
</msgs>
```

Note that the `error` attribute may contain `0` or `1`, and the `importance` attribute `low`, `medium`, or `high`.

Let us assume that we wish only to see those messages that are either errors (`error="1"`), or of high importance. We can select only these nodes for evaluation by referencing an XPath filter from the template, e.g.:

```
<xsl:apply-templates
  select="msg[@error='1' or @importance='high']"/>
```

The expression inside the square brackets is technically called a *predicate,* meaning function that returns a boolean value.

You can actually specify *multiple* filters within a single location path. For example, the XPath expression below specifies all cities in which live managers of companies that have share prices priced over $1:

```
/stock[@price > 1]/emp/name/[@mgmt = '1']/../address/city
```

Let's break this down: First we find all stock nodes that have `@price` elements larger than 1. From each of these stocks we consider all employees that have the management attribute set to 1. From each of those employees we navigate back from the name node and down to their address, and from there we gain their city of residence.

Note that we have used an implicit `number()` on our `@price` value.

Using Variables and Filters with Lookup Tables

In XSLT, as in many programming environments, we may want to have a table of name-value pairs. For example, we might want to obtain the string "Tuesday" from the value `3`. Variables and filters can be used together to obtain lookup-table functionality.

Suppose we wanted to display a list of dates with a format of "February 14, 1985", but are, instead, presented with a series of dates in the XML form:

```
<root>
  <dates>
    <date m="2" d="14" y="1985"/>
    <date m="7" d="8" y="1991"/>
    . . .
  <dates>
```

To translate the numeric values of months into the proper names of the months (1=January, 2=February, etc.), we will first need to establish a *lookup table* for converting numerical months to strings:

```
<months>
  <month id="1">January</month>
  <month id="2">February</month>
  <month id="3">March</month
```

```
    . . .
</months>
```

For the purpose of this example, we will assume that you have control over the XML input and can add the above months data as a child of the `root` element. (For those cases in which this is not possible you can use the `document()` XPath function to access a second XML input file from XSLT—see the CodeNotes website CN XM000504 for details.)

With our lookup table in place, we can build a rule for formatting the dates as required:

```
<xsl:template match="date">
  <xsl:variable name="m" select="@m"/>
  <xsl:value-of select="/root/months/month[@id=$m]"/>
  <xsl:value-of select="@d"/>,
  <xsl:value-of select="@y"/>
</xsl:template>
```

Listing 5.34   XPath logical operator existence examples

In Listing 5.34, we saved the `@m` attribute in a variable called `$m` (first boldface line) for use deep within an XPath expression (second boldface line). In the XPath expression we navigate all the way to the month nodeset, and from there select the month with an id equivalent to the value we saved in our variable, i.e., the value of this particular date. The `xsl:value-of plucks` out the month as text.

By adding a little additional HTML formatting, your output will appear in the browser as:

```
February 14, 1985
July 8, 1991
March 3, 1997
```

Regaining Context with current()

The example of Listing 5.34 used variables to save the context for use within an XPath expression. For a simple lookup, however, we can also use the `current()` function, along with string concatenation, to write the formatted date using one line of XSLT:

```
<xsl:value-of
select="concat(/root/months/month[@id=current()/@m],
' ', @d, ', ', @y)"/>
```

Let's study this line carefully. As in Listing 5.34 we are navigating to the month nodeset and selecting a particular month, but rather than looking up based on a value *saved* in a variable, we are regaining that value on the spot. We do so by calling `current()`, which returns the context node, a `date`. Once we have the date, it is simple to append `/@m` to gain the month.

Conditional Processing with xsl:if and xsl:choose

When you want to perform some operation conditionally, you need only make use of `xsf:if`. If, for example, you wanted to output the string "positive" when the attribute `distance` of the context node is a number larger than zero, you have:

```
<xsl:if test="@distance > 0">
  positive
</xsl:if>
```

Note that the `test` expression is actually a boolean XPath expression. `test` is a reserved word, and an explicit part of `xsl:if`.

If we wanted to output the string "negative, zero, or NaN" if `@distance` is smaller or equal to zero, or Not a Number (NaN) at all, we would have to use a second `xsl:if` with negated condition as follows:

```
<xsl:if test="not(@distance > 0)">
  negative, zero or NaN
</xsl:if>
```

Unfortunately XSLT does not support an `else` construct. To overcome this limitation, you can take advantage of `xsl:choose`:

```
<xsl:choose>
  <xsl:when test="@distance > 0 ">positive</xsl:when>
  <xsl:when test="@distance < 0">negative</xsl:when>
  <xsl:otherwise">zero or NaN</xsl:otherwise>
</xsl:if>
```

In this example, we have specified two `xsl:when` conditions within our `xsl:choose`, and we have taken advantage of the (optional) `xsl:otherwise`.

EXAMPLE

We'll use the instructions discussed in this topic and the data in Listing 5.35 to build a new, more powerful view of the data.

```
<?xml version="1.0"?
<job name="install signpost">
  <contractors>
    <contractor id="1">Jumbo Supplies</contractor>
    <contractor id="2">Thompson Fixtures</contractor>
    <contractor id="3">Bob's Hardware</contractor>
  </contractors>

  <specifics>
    <tools contractor_id ="3">
      <tool count="1">shovel</tool>
      <tool count="4">clamps</tool>
    </tools>

    <materials contractor_id ="1">
      <material amount="2 x 50lb">bag of cement</material>
      <material amount="15">screws</material>
      <material amount="2 x 1l">outdoor sealer</material>
    </materials>
  </specifics>
</job>
```

Listing 5.35 Construction job sample XML data

We would like to sort the job specifics by the text of the specific item (e.g., tool or material) or by contractor. We would also like to see the contractors listed with each specific item, as opposed to their IDs. Finally, we would like to color-code our output by contractor.

First, start a new XSLT document and add the following template:

```
<xsl:template match="/">
  <xsl:apply-templates select="job/specifics/*/*">
    <xsl:sort select="." data-type="text"/>
    <xsl:sort select="../@contractor_id" data-type="text"/>
  </xsl:apply-templates>
</xsl:template>
```

Listing 5.36 Part 1 of sorted rendering of data in 5.35

Above we are applying templates to all grandchildren (*/*) of job/specifics (tool and material nodes in our sample XML data). We are also sorting, first by tool or material, and second by contractor_id. Note that to specify sorting by contractor, we must access the parent (..) of the tool or material, and from there specify the contractor id.

Let's look at the bulk of the transform, which handles a particular tool or material:

```
<xsl:template match="*">
  <div>
    <xsl:attribute name="style">
      <xsl:choose>
      <xsl:when
          test="../@contractor_id='1'">color:blue</xsl:when>
      <xsl:when
          test="../@contractor_id='2'">color:green</xsl:when>
      <xsl:when
          test="../@contractor_id='3'">color:red</xsl:when>
      <xsl:otherwise>color:black</xsl:otherwise>
      </xsl:choose>
    </xsl:attribute>

    <xsl:value-of select="text()"/>
    (<xsl:value-of
      select="//contractor[@id=current()/../@contractor_id]"/>,
    <xsl:if test="@count">
      <xsl:value-of select="@count"/>
    </xsl:if>
    <xsl:if test="@amount">
      <xsl:value-of select="@amount"/>
    </xsl:if>)
  </div>
</xsl:template>
```

Listing 5.37 Part 2 of sorted rendering of data in 5.35

In the above example we color each row using xsl:attribute, which creates a style on the div element with a particular color. The color was selected based on the @contractor_id of the node above—we used xsl:choose to select a particular color. Note that if the colors were available in a list indexed by contractor id, we could have collapsed the selection into a single lookup. (See Listing 5.34 for an example of this technique.)

Using the `xsl:value-of` (shown in bold), we did a lookup to retrieve the contractor name from the id—as in several previous examples, we used `current()` to regain our context in order to specify a condition for the filter that selects the contractor name.

Sample output in IE is shown below. To instead sort first by contractor id, we would just have to swap the `xsl:sort lines` in Listing 5.36.

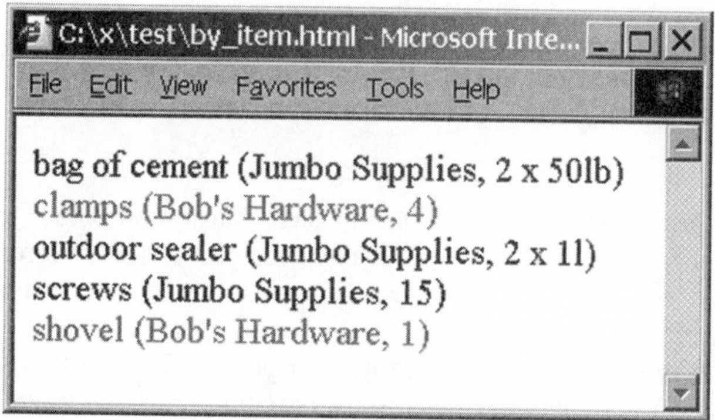

Figure 5.6 Output of Listing 5.30 and 5.31 applied to data in 5.12

HOW AND WHY

Can I Sort on Multiple Keys?

Yes. List the keys starting with the most important in multiple `xsl:sort elements.` For example:

```
<xsl:sort data-type="last"/>
<xsl:sort data-type="first"/>
```

The above sorts by last name, and then by first name, much like a telephone directory.

BUGS AND CAVEATS

Sorting by Time, Date, Etc.

XSLT 1.0 supports sorting by string and by number only. However, a number of alternatives exist to sort by date or on some other data type. A list of these alternatives follows, ordered from most to least preferable:

1. Represent dates in numerical year-month-day format (e.g., 2001-05-25), and sort as text. Be sure to pad the day and month to two digits, and the year to four. Otherwise, for example, 2001-5-25 would be considered greater than 2001-10-25.
2. Maintain multiple representations in your source XML—one for sorting, another for processing or display. For example:

```
< . . . >
  <yymmdd_date>2001 05 25</yymmdd_date>
  <display_date>May 25, 1972</display_date>
< . . . >
```

   Here you would display `display_date`, but sort on `yymmdd_date`.
3. In the `select` attribute of `xsl:sort`, derive a sortable expression from the given input (essentially, within XSLT, descramble the dates you are provided).
4. Sort the XML elements before you present them to the XSLT processor, or alternatively sort the output of the XSLT transform.

The recently published specification for XML schemas (discussed in Chapter 8), combined with a future version of XSLT, will likely provide first-class sorting behavior on commonly used data types, such as dates and times.

DESIGN NOTES

Use Constants for Legibility

Avoid embedding numerical values in your XSLT. For example, the following code:

```
<xsl:if test="date=7 or date=1">
  <p>warning, weekend appointment</p>
</xsl:if>
```

would be easier to read and maintain as:

```
<xsl:variable name="SUNDAY" select="1"/>
<xsl:variable name="MONDAY" select="2"/>
<!--  . . .  -->

<xsl:if test="date=$SATURDAY or date=$SUNDAY">  . . .
```

SUMMARY

We've examined some extremely useful tools in this topic. XPath filters such as stock `[@trading="1" and @price > 50]` are extremely powerful, and make it possible to create output that is significantly different from the input.

By allowing us to choose what is executed and what is not at transform time, `xsl:if` and `xsl:choose` further enrich our output by providing multiple views on a dataset, selectable by the user.

Finally, we have moved beyond simple list processing and into more general lookups, as we did with the month name lookup in Listing 5.34.

Topic: Working with Templates

Templates can be said to be the core of XSLT. Now that we have a firm grounding in XPath and various output techniques, we'll examine more sophisticated features of templates. We will first explore *recursive templates* (templates that call themselves to process arbitrarily nested input). By "arbitrarily nested" we mean an element or set of elements that contains itself as a child. Think of an XML input representing a menu, for example.

We'll also demonstrate how *named templates* enable reuse, in much the same way as functions in a programming language.

Finally, we'll demonstrate what to do when your XSLT files get too large to handle; by splitting XSLT stylesheets into multiple XSLT files you make your development project easier to manage, permit a team-based approach and promote reuse.

CONCEPTS

Recursive Templates

Consider building a treelike HTML menu for a website. Rather than hard-coding the menu options directly in HTML, it is preferable to make our menu options changeable by encoding the menu options in XML and delivering the HTML via XSLT. Examine the following XML:

```
<?xml version="1.0"?>
<menu>
```

```
  <mi name="Emergency Shutdown!"/>
  <mi name="Analyze">
    <mi name="Portfolio"/>
    <mi name="Market"/>
    <mi name="Competition"/>
  </mi>
  <mi name="Operations">
    <mi name="Buy"/>
    <mi name="Sell"/>
  </mi>
</menu>
```

Listing 5.38 Recursive input

To process the XML in Listing 5.38, we use named templates—`xsl:for-each` cannot process arbitrarily nested elements such as `<mi>`.

```
<xsl:template match="/menu">
  <xsl:apply-templates select="mi"/>
</xsl:template>

<xsl:template match="mi">
  <div style="margin-left:20px"><xsl:value-of select="@name"/>
    <xsl:apply-templates select="mi"/>
  </div>
</xsl:template>
```

Listing 5.39 Recursive processing

Notice that the second rule has an `xsl:apply-templates` instruction itself. This instruction applies templates to any `mi` *children* of the current context, which just happens to be an `mi` itself. In other words, the `mi` template *recurses*. Run this example and view the output in your browser—you should see something like this:

```
Emergency Shutdown!
Analyze
   Portfolio
   Market
   Competition
Operations
   Buy
   Sell
```

That's a good start on our menu. For an example of a complete, functional DHTML menu encoded in XSLT, see the CodeNotes website CN XM000590.

Declaring and Calling Reusable Named Templates

Up until this point we've seen templates evaluated *implicitly*—that is, based on the `match` attribute. In addition to using match, we can also specify a `name` for the template, which allows us *explicit* evaluation. A named template is very similar to a function, which has a name and may be called based on that name.

Consider the following problem that a named template can help solve—your XML input file actually specifies how some data (coming from the input file) is to be formatted by your XSL file. For the purpose of this example, imagine you are required to format a value to a number of decimal places specified by your input XML document. For example, you are given:

```
<price decimals="4" value="123.948760"/>
```

If we knew ahead of time that the value attribute needed to be formatted to four decimal places, we could have hard-coded a format string like `#,##0.0000` and used the function `format-number() function`. We do not, however, know how we will need to format the value until our template processes the price element. It is only when we retrieve the decimals attribute that we will know how to format the number held by the value attribute. To format on the fly, we need to create a format string, such as `#,##0.0000`, *dynamically*. Although it may seem straightforward, it is difficult to create a string with the number of zeros as specified in `@decimals`.

XSLT does not directly support iterating a fixed number of times. While there is `xsl:for-each`, there is no FOR..NEXT construct. Therefore, to build the above format string on the fly, we must resort to what is called *tail recursion*. In tail recursion, a recursive template applies children as its last operation, which then calls the template again (recursion). This is as close as XSLT comes to supporting a simple loop.

Because this process is rather cumbersome, we will wrap it up in a named template called `copies`. The named template in Listing 5.40 may be difficult to follow, so don't worry if it doesn't make complete sense upon first reading:

```
<xsl:template name="copies">
  <xsl:param name="x"/>
```

```
  <xsl:param name="count"/>
  <xsl:value-of select="$x"/>
  <xsl:if test="$count > 1">
    <xsl:call-template name="copies">
      <xsl:with-param name="x" select="$x"/>
      <xsl:with-param name="count" select="($count) - 1"/>
    </xsl:call-template>
  </xsl:if>
</xsl:template>
```

Listing 5.40 Copy function to make $count copies of $x

The XSLT in Listing 5.40 demonstates both:

1. How to declare a named template (first line) that accepts parameters (second and third lines). The parameters act exactly like the variables we have encountered previously.
2. How to call a named template (first line of inner bold block) with parameters (remaining lines of inner bold block).

Since even *calling* a named template with several parameters is somewhat messy, it can simplify things to wrap the `xsl:call-template` in a variable as shown in Listing 5.41:

```
<xsl:variable name="zeroes">
  <xsl:call-template name="copies">
    <xsl:with-param name="x" select="0"/>
    <xsl:with-param name="count" select="@decimals"/>
  </xsl:call-template>
</xsl:variable>
```

Listing 5.41 Calling the copy function

Now, with this infrastructure in place, we can output our `value` formatted to `@decimals` places using the `$zeroes` variable:

```
format-number(number(value), concat("#,##0.", $zeroes))
```

Including Other Files and Template Priorities

In development XSLT, you will often want to include one XSLT file within another. This is simple to do: just place `xsl:include` at the top level of your XSLT:

```
<xsl:include href="base.xsl"/>
```

EXAMPLE

Way back in Listing 5.27 we presented a simple function for translating English-character-only strings to uppercase. This kind of reusable functionality is ideal for packaging up in a named template:

```
<xsl:template name="makeUpper">
  <xsl:param name="s"/>
  <xsl:value-of select="translate(s,
  'abcdefghijklmnopqrstuvwxyz',
  'ABCDEFGHIJKLMNOPQRSTUVWXYZ')"/>
</xsl:template>
```

Listing 5.42 Reusable English-character-only case conversion

Of course, you could construct `makeLower` by simply switching the two strings of the alphabet. If we wanted to make use of `makeUpper` to make an important warning uppercase, we would use:

```
<xsl:call-template name="makeUpper">
  <xsl:with-param name="s" select="fatalError"/>
</xsl:call-template>
```

Listing 5.43 Calling makeUpper with contents of fatalError

If you did not want to output the value, but instead place it into a variable (perhaps for comparison against a stock set of errors for special handling), you could wrap the template call in a variable, as in:

```
<xsl:variable name="fatalErrorUC">
  <xsl:call-template name="makeUpper">
    <xsl:with-param name="s" select="fatalError"/>
  </xsl:call-template>
</xsl:variable>
```

Listing 5.44 Storing result of call to makeUpper with fatalError in variable $fatalErrorUC.

Now you may use the variable `$fatalErrorUC` in an `xsl:value-of`, as a parameter to another named template, and so on.

SUMMARY

XSLT supports what is commonly called "programming in-the-large"—or constructs that help make larger projects more manageable.

Named templates, created by specifying a `name` attribute on an `xsl:template` element, provide a different approach from simply matching templates to input, allowing us to create a reusable base of utility functions independent of a particular input grammar. In this chapter, we also investigated techniques for sharing XSLT among one or several files, as large teams cannot work from a single file.

Additional features providing much-needed flexibility when working on larger projects are template *modes* CN XML000505 and template *priorities* CN XML000506.

Chapter Summary

XSLT is a compact and powerful technology for transforming XML data. Using the functionality outlined in this chapter alone, you will be able to construct substantial systems with XSLT transformations as the backbone. This presents a very attractive addition to, and often replacement for, conventional programming-language-based data processing.

Chapter 6

PROGRAMMING WITH DOM

The Document Object Model (DOM) is a W3C standard for reading and manipulating XML data. As with SAX (discussed in the next chapter) you can choose from various parser implementations of DOM (with corresponding APIs). Regardless of which DOM parser you choose, DOM presents an XML document as a tree of *nodes,* where each node represents an element, attribute, or text data. The tree structure that the DOM creates will always correspond to the hierarchical structure of the XML document it is used to parse. The root element (or node) sits on the first level of the tree, its children on the next level, and so on. The DOM provides random access to any of these nodes, which means that you can read or change any part of the document at any time.

The sample applications in this chapter are written in Java and Visual Basic to emphasize the similarities between DOM-based applications, regardless of the language or platform used. The mechanics of using DOM with Perl and JavaScript are covered in CodeNotes Pointers CN XM00016 and CN XM000107, respectively.

The various W3C specifications for DOM are located at http://www.w3.org/DOM/DOMTR. This CodeNote covers the most recent recommendation at the time of this writing, DOM Level 2.

SIMPLE APPLICATION

The following simple applications require the XML document in Listing 6.1, `hello.xml`:

```
<?xml version="1.0"?>
<display>Hello World!</display>
```

Listing 6.1 hello.xml

Note that each sample requires an installed DOM parser for the language you wish to use. See the XML Parsers section in Chapter 2 (Installation) for details.

Java (Using the DOM Parser Included in JAXP)

To demonstrate how the DOM parser operates, save the file shown in Listing 6.2 as `hello.java` and compile with the command "`javac hello.java`". The `hello.java` program loads `hello.xml` into memory using the DOM, and outputs the contents of the `<display>` element to the console.

```
import javax.xml.parsers.*;
import org.w3c.dom.*;

public class hello {
  public static void main(String[] argv) {
    try {
      // load and parse the document
      DocumentBuilder builder;
      DocumentBuilderFactory factory =
          DocumentBuilderFactory.newInstance();
      builder = factory.newDocumentBuilder();
      Document document = builder.parse("hello.xml");

      // retrieve and display Hello World!
      Element root = document.getDocumentElement();
      Node text = root.getFirstChild();
      System.out.println(text.getNodeValue());
    } catch(Exception e) { // removed for brevity
    } // try
  } // main
} // hello
```

Listing 6.2 Java + DOM Hello World (hello.java)

To run the Java Hello World example, ensure that `parser.jar` and `jaxp.jar` are in your `CLASSPATH`, and that `hello.xml` is in the same directory as `hello.class`.

The output of the Java Hello World application is shown in Listing 6.3.

```
Hello World!
```

Listing 6.3 Output of hello.java, from Listing 6.2

Visual Basic (Using the DOM Parser Included in MSXML3)

In Visual Basic, create a Standard EXE with Listing 6.4 as code for the `Form_Load()` method in `Form1`. This code displays the contents of `hello.xml`'s `<display>` element in a message box.

```
Option Explicit

Private Sub Form_Load()
  Dim doc As New DOMDocument
  Dim root As IXMLDOMElement
  Dim text As IXMLDOMText

  ' load and parse hello.xml
  doc.Load "file:c:\temp\hello.xml"

  ' retrieve and print Hello World!
  Set root = doc.documentElement
  Set text = root.firstChild
  Msgbox text.nodeValue
End Sub
```

Listing 6.4 VB Hello World

Under VB's Project | References menu dialogue, add a reference to "Microsoft XML 3.0" (MSXML3.DLL). Move the `hello.xml` file to the directory listed in the `doc.Load` command (`c:\temp` in Listing 6.4). It is important that you use the full path name to `hello.xml`, as relative paths can be troublesome when developing in VB. For more information on the `Load` method and paths, see CodeNotes Pointer CN XML000507.

When you run the application, you should see a message box that says: "Hello World".

CORE CONCEPTS

When to Use DOM

You should use the DOM when you require full, random access to the contents of an XML document, as is often the case with document-oriented programs. For example, consider writing a program that allows the user to interact with a spreadsheet of data stored in an XML file. You might use the DOM to represent that data in memory. DOM also supports methods for changing the structure of a loaded document, such as adding a new element. Many DOM implementations also offer nonstandard but very useful functionality, such as saving documents and returning nodesets from XPath expressions (discussed in Chapter 5).

DOM's main disadvantage is that it loads an entire document into memory. If you are working with especially large documents, or only require fast, one-pass access to the contents of an XML document, you should instead investigate using SAX (Chapter 7) as an alternative. SAX-based programs process an XML document by working with small fragments one at a time (an element, some text, etc.), and, as a result, tend to be much faster and less memory-intensive than the DOM-based applications.

Loading a Document

At the time of writing, the W3C has not standardized an API for loading an XML document and "kicking off" the parsing process; instead, each implementation has a proprietary way of starting the parsing process. The following examples illustrate methods for loading XML files using the DOM with Java (using the JAXP package) and Visual Basic (using MSXML3). Most other DOM implementations follow one of these two basic patterns.

Java (JAXP)

Java uses a "factory" pattern to generate a new instance of a parser, which can then be used to create the DOM document. The factory pattern provides a layer of abstraction between the code and the actual implementation, allowing you to switch parsers without significantly changing your code.

The Java code of Listing 6.5 uses JAXP DOM to load a document and begin the parsing processes:

```
//Assumes import of org.w3c.dom.* and javax.xml.parsers.*
try {
  DocumentBuilder builder;
```

```
    DocumentBuilderFactory factory =
        DocumentBuilderFactory.newInstance();
    builder = factory.newDocumentBuilder();

    Document document = builder.parse(filenameAsAString);
  } catch (Exception e) {
    //can throw several exceptions, including IOException
  }
```

Listing 6.5 Using JAXP and DOM to load a document

The `DocumentBuilderFactory` is used to create a new `Doucument-Builder`. `DocumentBuilder` is actually an abstraction of a DOM parser. The `parse()` method of the `DocumentBuilder` object (variable `builder` in the code above) loads and parses the XML file, returning a `Document` object that holds the contents of the entire XML file in memory.

Visual Basic (MSXML3)

The following VB code loads a document using Microsoft's DOM implementation, MSXML3:

```
Dim doc As New DOMDocument
doc.Load filenameAsAString

If doc.parseError.errorCode <> 0 Then
  MsgBox "An error occurred while parsing"
End If
```

Listing 6.6 Using VB's DOMDocument to load an XML document

Unlike the Java and JAXP implementation, MSXML3 extends the standard DOM document interface by adding the `Load()` method for opening a document.

Document Storage

The DOM presents an XML document as a tree. You can also think of it as a recursive list of lists. Your application processes the XML by navigating the DOM tree—enumerating children, finding parents, etc. For example, consider a simple XML file and its DOM representation:

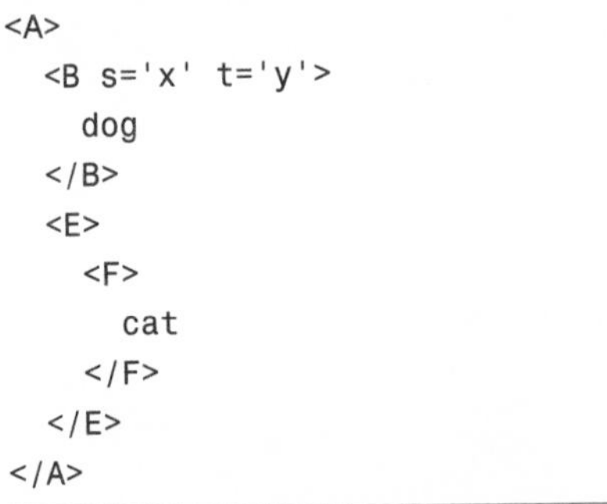

```
<A>
  <B s='x' t='y'>
    dog
  </B>
  <E>
    <F>
      cat
    </F>
  </E>
</A>
```

Listing 6.7 letters.xml

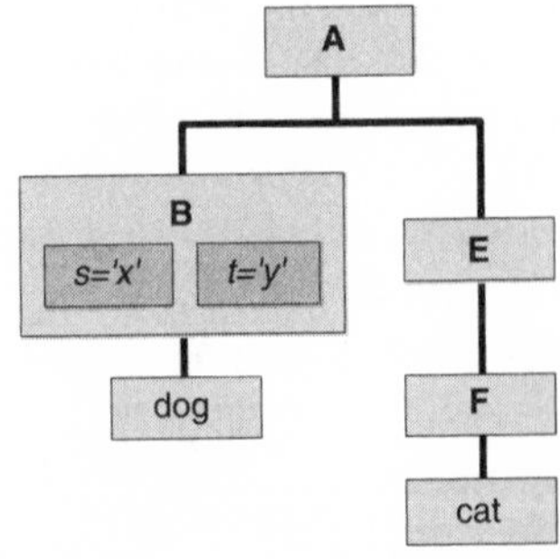

Figure 6.1 DOM representation

The DOM presents a tree consisting entirely of *nodes*. There are three primary types of nodes: *element nodes* (which may have text and element child nodes, as well as attributes), *text nodes*, and *attribute nodes*. Text and attribute nodes are sometimes called *leaf nodes;* they have no children, as leaves on a tree have no branches.

In Figure 6.1, the element A, for example, has two children, elements B and E. Element E has one child, element F, which has one child text node containing the string "cat". Element B holds one child text node ("dog") and two attribute nodes, s and t. The s and t nodes contain the values "x" and "y" respectively. Attributes are not considered element children, and are accessed differently from child elements or text nodes.

Depending on the parser configuration and vendor, there may, in fact, be additional nodes representing *ignorable whitespace*. In Figure 6.1, node A might have three additional text node children representing the new line (carriage return) characters between each of its child elements. The MSXML3 DOM implementation does not expose these nodes by default (though you may override this behavior using the `DOMDocument.preserveWhiteSpace` property). On the other hand, the JAXP DOM will present these nodes by default.

It is important to distinguish between *children* and *descendants*. For example, in Figure 6.1, B and E are children of A, while B, E and F are descendants. Likewise, we can distinguish between *parents* and *ancestors*. In Figure 6.1, E is the parent of F, but both A and E are ancestors. Finally, an element's *siblings* are the children of its parent. In Figure 6.1, B and E are siblings, as they share a common parent, A.

Performance

DOM parsers operate by reading an entire XML document into memory, and presenting this data to your application as a tree. Although a DOM parser may permit *asynchronous* operation (allowing your application to execute unrelated code while the parsing continues), the tree will not be available until the parse operation is complete. The necessity of parsing an XML file before working with the file has the following implications:

- You cannot interrupt or cancel the parser mid-operation.
- The entire document is held in memory. As a very approximate rule of thumb, a DOM parser uses two to ten times as much memory as the size of the original XML document (depending on the exact proportion of node types).

For these reasons, DOM may not be well suited for parsing very large documents. In these circumstances, you may need to consider a SAX parser, discussed in Chapter 7 (Programming with SAX).

Asynchronous Support in MSXML3

Microsoft's latest implementation of the DOM parser (MSMXL3) offers an asynchronous processing feature. If you are loading large documents and do not wish to "freeze" your user interface while doing so, you may choose to set the `DOMDocument async` property to true before calling `load()` or `loadXML()`. You must then occasionally check the document `ReadyState` property, or better yet trap the `onreadystatechange` event. See the CodeNotes website CN XM000677 for examples of both approaches.

Classes

The DOM defines several critical class objects, providing all of the basic functionality for accessing the DOM tree. The DOM class hierarchy is illustrated in Figure 6.2.

The arrows in Figure 6.2 indicate *inheritance* (the arrow points from the derived class to the more general base class). The diagram lists only the methods that are used when navigating a document. Additional methods (e.g., creating new nodes) will be discussed later in this chapter.

Note that the class names represent the actual DOM standard. Certain implementations (most notably Microsoft's MSXML) use different names. For example, a `Node` is actually named `IXMLDOMNode` in Visual Basic.

Node Classes

Every node in the DOM tree is either an `Element`, `Text`, or `Attr` node. Each of these classes is derived from the `Node` class, which provides generic access to any object in the XML DOM tree.

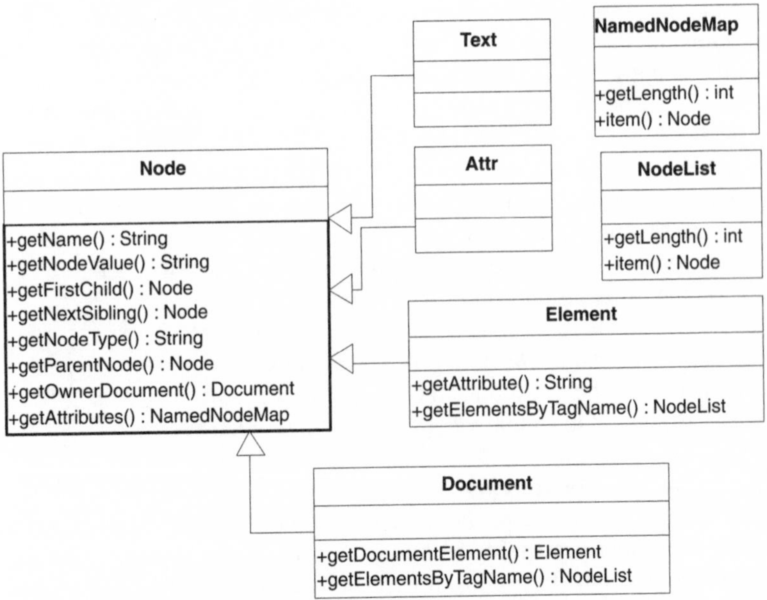

Figure 6.2 The class hierarchy for the DOM

In the earlier `letters.xml` example of Listing 6.7, Nodes `A`, `B`, `E`, and `F` would be represented as `Element` objects; Nodes `s` and `t` as `Attr` objects; and the Nodes containing `cat` and `dog` are `Text` objects.

While you can work exclusively with `Node objects`, it is often more convenient to *downcast* to one of the derived types to take advantage of special behavior. For example, consider the following nonoptimal code:

```
// assumes myNode is a valid Node object, with child element
// named "child1", with attribute id
Node child = myNode.getFirstChild();
System.out.println("The id of child1 is: "
    + child.getAttributes().getNamedItem("id").getValue());
```

Listing 6.8 Working with nodes

If we know that the first child is actually an `Element` object, we can simplify the last line of this example (in bold) by downcasting directly to an `Element`:

```
// assumes myNode is a valid Node object, with child element
// named "child1", with attribute id
```

```
Element child = (Element)myNode.getFirstChild();
System.out.println("The id of child1 is: "
    + child.getAttribute("id"));
```

Listing 6.9 Downcasting to an element

Where Java forces you to explicitly downcast, Visual Basic hides the downcast. For example, a Visual Basic equivalent listing to 6.9 would be:

```
Dim child as IXMLDomElement
Set child = myNode.firstChild
MsgBox "The id of child1 is: " & child.getAttribute("id")
```

Listing 6.10 Downcasting in Visual Basic

In all three cases, the `getFirstChild()` method returns a `Node` object (the parent class) that may be downcast (or converted) to the appropriate child class (i.e., `Element`). Downcasting and node types are further explained in the Document Navigation topic.

Node Collections

The DOM also defines two collection objects, `NodeList` and `NamedNodeMap`. `NodeList` contains an ordered group of element and text nodes, and is returned by many functions such as `getChildNodes()`. The `NamedNodeMap` collection contains attribute name/value pairs, and is returned by functions such as `getAttributes()`.

Both collections share two functions: `item()` and `length()`. `NamedNodeMap` has additional functions for retrieving the value of a specifically named node. Be aware that different implementations use these collections differently. For example, Java uses a `NodeIterator` object to move through the `NodeList`, while Visual Basic has iteration methods built into the `IXMLNodeList` object.

Threading Models

JAXP

The `DocumentBuilder` class is *not* thread-safe, which means you cannot concurrently parse multiple files using the DOM.

MSXML3

MSXML3 actually provides multiple document objects, each possessing different threading abilities. For example, `DOMDocument` supports what, in Microsoft's Component Object Model (COM), is called the

Apartment model. There is another object known as FreeThreaded DOMDocument that supports the Free Threaded model. A detailed discussion of COM threading models is beyond the scope of this CodeNote. See *Applying COM+*, Chapter 4 (Gregory Brill, New Riders Publishing, Indianapolis, 2000), for a breakdown of the different threading models. Briefly, however, an Apartment model object is inherently thread-safe; all method invocations from any thread are serialized into the object via a hidden message queue. For this, and more subtle reasons, you should use DOMDocument when working with single-threaded versions of Visual Basic (VB6 and lower). The FreeThreaded-DOMDocument object allows access by any thread. This may provide better performance with certain clients than DOMDocument. However, this is not a firm rule. Some clients actually show faster performance with DOMDocument. When in doubt, choose DOMDocument instead of FreeThreadedDOMDocument.

Topic: Document Navigation

Navigating a document using the DOM is a straightforward exercise. This topic will demonstrate the traversal of a document node by node. In other words, you will see how to move through a parsed DOM tree and look at each element in turn.

You will also learn how to extract all elements with a given tag name. You might, for example, wish to retrieve all periodical elements from an XML file containing a number of publications.

The methods used to manipulate a document, (i.e., adding, deleting, and modifying nodes) are discussed in the next topic, Document Manipulation.

As a reminder, the examples in this chapter are written in Java; however, methods in other implementations of the DOM, such as MSXML, will have a very similar structure. Differences are noted as appropriate.

CONCEPTS

Retrieving the Root Node

The DOM refers to the root node as the *document element*. To obtain the root node, use getDocumentElement():

```
//doc is an org.w3c.dom.document object
Element root = doc.getDocumentElement();
```

Listing 6.11 The Document.getDocument() method

To obtain the root from any node in the DOM:

```
//any is any Node object (Element, text, attr)
Element root = any.getOwnerDocument().getDocumentElement();
```

Listing 6.12 Using the Node.getOwnerDocument() method

Retrieving Child and Parent Elements

Once you have a starting point, such as the root node, you can use `getFirstChild()` to retrieve the first child node. Additional methods such as `getNextSibling()` allow you to iterate to the next node in the list. These methods are illustrated in Listing 6.13, which walks down a DOM tree, recursively processing each node it encounters:

```
//assumes import of org.w3c.dom.*
private static void processNodes(Node curNode) {
  Node curChild = curNode.getFirstChild();

  // loop through all immediate children
  While (curChild != null) {
    // perform processing steps here

    // recursive call to access children
    processNodes(curChild);
    curChild = curChild.getNextSibling();
  } // while
} // processNodes
```

Listing 6.13 Recursively processing nodes on a DOM tree

The code shown in Listing 6.13 loops through all child `text` and `element` nodes of `curNode` in the order in which they appear in the document. Recursive code can sometimes be tricky to read, but you might want to trace through the code of Listing 6.13 to satisfy yourself that it will, in fact, traverse an entire DOM tree. This code will not, however, accommodate attributes. Remember that attribute nodes are not children of the current node; therefore, they are not included in `processNodes()`'s traversal. Accessing attributes is discussed in the upcoming topic, Working with Attributes.

Should you ever wish to backtrack from a particular node up the tree to reach its ancestors, use `Node.getParentNode()`:

```
//curNode is a valid Node, element or text object
Node parent = curNode.getParentNode();
```

Listing 6.14 The Node.getParentNode() method

Because attributes are not considered children of elements, `Node.getParentNode()` returns `null` when used on `Attr` objects. `Document` objects also return `null` as their parent node (after all, the document is the top level parent node).

Node Types

When using the DOM to navigate through lists of nodes, you will often wish to determine the actual type of a given node; is it an element, text, document, or attribute? You might, for example, wish to downcast a node to an element only when the node is, in fact, an element.

In Java, the `Node` class has a method (`getNodetype()`) that returns a constant indicating the node type. These constants are available as members of the `Node` class, so you don't have to worry about integer numbers.

In Visual Basic, the `IXMLDOMNode` interface exposes a `nodeType` property, which returns one of the values in the `DOMNodeType` enumeration.

Listing 6.15 demonstrates one approach (in Java) to determine a node's type and downcast appropriately:

```
// node is an object of type Node
switch(node.getNodeType()) {
  case Node.ELEMENT_NODE:
    Element element = (Element)node;
    // process element
    break;
  case Node.TEXT_NODE:
    Text text = (Text)node;
    // process text node
    break;
  default:
  // default handling
}
```

Listing 6.15 Determining a node's type

See the CodeNotes website CN XM000678 for a similar example using Visual Basic.

Working with Attributes

Attribute values may be retrieved by name using the `Element` interface as shown in Listing 6.16.

```
//elem is a org.w3c.dom.Element object
String price = elem.getAttribute("price");
```

Listing 6.16 Accessing an attribute value

The code in Listing 6.16 finds the value of the element `elem`'s `price` attribute and stores it in a string named `price`.

For documents with elements containing many attributes, it may be preferable to loop through all attributes rather than retrieve them individually by name:

```
//element is a valid Node, text or element object
NamedNodeMap nnm = elem.getAttributes();
// NamedNodeMap is a 0-based collection
int i = 0;
while (i < nnm.getLength()) {
  // NamedNodeMap stores Nodes,
  Attr curAtt = (Attr)nnm.item(i);
  // process curAtt
  i++;
}
```

Listing 6.17 Iterating through the attributes of an element

Note that you have to explicitly downcast the output of the `NamedNodeMap` object (`nnm`) to the `Attr` class.

Unlike text and element children, the DOM makes no guarantee that the ordering of attributes in a `NamedNodeMap` matches that of the original XML document. The attributes can be in any order, and the order may be different every time you retrieve a `NamedNodeMap`.

Searching Globally

Situations will inevitably arise where you will want to retrieve a group of related elements without needing to traverse the tree. Fortunately, the `Document` and `Element` classes contain the convenient `getElementsByTagName()` method. This method will retrieve all instances of the named element that are below (descendants of) the current node (used to call the method). For `Document` objects (remember, a `Document` object represents the entire XML document), calling the `getElementsByTagName()` method will retrieve all elements in the entire document with the given tag name.

Listing 6.18 illustrates the `getElementsByTagName()` method by retrieving all `<book>` elements from the document level:

```
//doc is an org.w3c.dom.Document object
NodeList elemList = doc.getElementsByTagName("book");
for (int i=0; i < elemList.getLength(); i++) {
  Node curElem = elemList.item(i);
  // add processing code here
} // for
```

Listing 6.18 Using the Document.getElementsByTagName() method

Notice that `getElementsByTagName()` returns a `NodeList` containing the nodes in the order they appear within the original XML file.

Retrieving Node Information

Once you have found the node you were searching for, you will inevitably want to retrieve information from it. The DOM defines two generic functions for returning the name of the node (`getName()`) and the node value (`getNodeValue()`). These methods work with both text nodes and element nodes (which may, in turn, have attributes and child nodes). Depending on the node type being accessed, `getNodeValue()` will return values as described in Table 6.1:

Node Type	Returned Value
Attribute	The value of the attribute
Element	`Null`
Document	`Null`
Text	The value of the text string

Table 6.1 Results of Node.getNodeValue() by node type

When `getNodeValue()` does return a value, it is always a `string`. For example, to retrieve the text contained within a text node, use the code in Listing 6.19.

```
String text = textNode.getNodeValue();
```

Listing 6.19 Using the Node.getNodeValue() method

The `Node.getName()` method returns the name of an element or attribute. An element of type `<book>` has a name, unsurprisingly, of `book`, for example. For text and document nodes, `getName()` always returns the hard-coded values of `#text` and `#document`, respectively.

```
String tagName = elem.getName();
```

Listing 6.20 Using the Node.getName() method

Note that an element's name will always include any namespace prefixes. For example, an XML `<book>` element that was associated with (or in) the namespace `history` (i.e. `<history:book>`) will return the value "`history:book`" when `getName()` is used to find its value.

EXAMPLE

Generating Formatted XML

The DOM specification does not specify methods that take in an element name and will return the entire tree underneath it in a `NodeList`. This is often a necessary task when working with the DOM.

Listing 6.21 provides source code for the `showTree()` function, which demonstrates how one might display the entire contents of an XML file starting from any particular node. Note that `showTree()` is a recursive function and operates on all descendants of a given node:

```
//assumes import of org.w3c.dom.*
private static void showTree(Node curNode) {
  System.out.print("<" + curNode.getNodeName() + " ");

  // process attributes
  NamedNodeMap nnm = curNode.getAttributes();
  int i=0;
  while (i < nnm.getLength()) {
    Attr curAtt = (Attr)nnm.item(i);
    String text = curAtt.getNodeName() + "=\"" +
        curAtt.getNodeValue() + "\"";
    System.out.print(text + " ");
    i++;
  } // while
  System.out.println(">");

  // process child nodes
  Node curChild = curNode.getFirstChild();
  while (curChild != null) {
    if (Node.TEXT_NODE == curChild.getNodeType()) {
      String textValue = curChild.getNodeValue().trim();
```

```
      // ignore whitespace in the XML file
      if (textValue.length() > 0 ) {
        System.out.println("'" + textValue + "'");
      } // if
    } else if (Node.ELEMENT_NODE == curChild.getNodeType()) {
      showTree(curChild);     // recursive call
    } // if
    curChild = curChild.getNextSibling();
  } // while
  System.out.println("</" + curNode.getNodeName() + ">");
} // showTree
```

Listing 6.21 Source code for the showTree() function

The `showTree()` method in Listing 6.21 loops over all the attributes in a given element, and then recursively through all of the child nodes. As text nodes and attributes cannot have children, the values for these nodes are printed, but no further recursive calls are necessary. Note that whitespace in the XML file is ignored. See CN XM000679 for the equivalent example in Visual Basic.

Retrieving the Price of a Stock from an XML File

We conclude this topic with a quick example demonstrating how a particular element can be found and its data retrieved from an XML document. Assume the XML file in Listing 6.22 stores stock prices, names, and symbols:

```
<?xml version="1.0"?>
<stocks>
  <stock price="50.25">
    <name>International Business Machines</name>
    <symbol>IBM</symbol>
  </stock>
  <!-- repeats for the rest of the stocks-->
</stocks>
```

Listing 6.22 Sample format for storing stock prices

To search for a particular stock by its symbol name and retrieve the price for that particular stock, consider:

```
private static float getPrice(Document doc, String stockSymbol)
{
```

```
  NodeList symbols = doc.getElementsByTagName("symbol");

  // search according to stock symbol
  for (int i = 0; i < symbols.getLength(); i++) {
    // cast from Nodes to refined class
    Element curSym = (Element)symbols.item(i);
    Text symbol = (Text)curSym.getFirstChild();
    if (symbol.getNodeValue().equals(stockSymbol)) {
      // found the stock, return price as a float
      Element stock = (Element)curSym.getParentNode();
      String price = stock.getAttribute("price");
      return new Float(price).floatValue();
    } // if
  } // for
  // didn't find price, return error value
  return -1.0f;
}
```

Listing 6.23 Source code for the getPrice() method

In `getPrice()`, we first find all of the stock symbol elements and store them in a `NodeList` (named `symbols`). We then iterate through `symbols` and compare each symbol value in the list to the desired stock symbol (which is a parameter of the `getPrice()` function, named `stockSymbol`). Once we have found the matching symbol, we retrieve the parent element (a `stock` element) to get the price element. See CN `XM000680` for equivalent Visual Basic source code.

The `getPrice()` method in Listing 6.23 can be used to obtain the current price for an IBM as shown in Listing 6.24.

```
float price = getPrice(document, "IBM");
System.out.println(Float.toString(price));
```

Listing 6.24 Using the getPrice method

HOW AND WHY

Does the DOM Treat <a/> the Same as <a></a>?

Yes it does; in both cases the element `a` is an empty node and has no child nodes.

How are Mixed Elements Represented?

Mixed elements (elements with both text and element children) maintain their structure using DOM. For example, the fragment `<a>Howdy<b/>There</a>` is represented by DOM as shown in Figure 6.3.

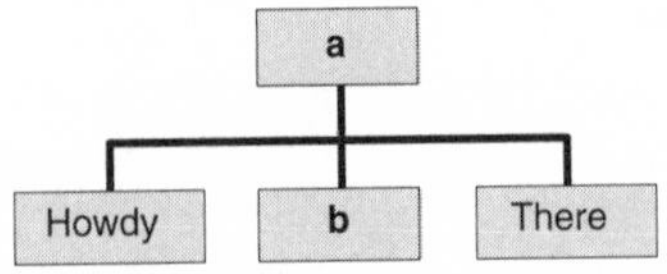

Figure 6.3 The DOM representation of a mixed element

Notice that the text nodes, `Howdy` and `There`, are siblings of the element node `<b/>`. In other words, all three nodes are children of `<a>`.

Can I Use XPath with the DOM?

XPath is the compact query language described in Chapter 5. The DOM Level 2 standard does not support XPath queries on documents because the W3C group developing the DOM was not completely satisfied with XPath as a querying language. However, it is expected that DOM Level 3, when released, will provide standardized support for XPath, as no other XML query languages have been fully developed.

MSXML3 does, however, provide extension methods supporting an XPath query on a document node:

```
'This is Visual Basic Code
'returns the first node that would
'be selected by the given XPath query
Dim Node As IXMLDOMNode
'Assume Node has been assigned a valid node object
Node.selectSingleNode(strXPath)

'returns a NodeList of all nodes
'matching the given XPath query
Node.selectNodes(strXPath)
```

Listing 6.25 Methods in MSXML3 that support XPath

This is extremely powerful functionality for applications that search for particular nodes, or calculate aggregate values such as totals and averages. Examples can be found on the CodeNotes website CN XM000601.

How Do I Work with Namespaces When Navigating?

The DOM methods for working with namespaces are quite similar to the normal methods that do not recognize namespaces. All methods for working with namespaces have the suffix `NS` and otherwise function in the same manner as the corresponding methods without the `NS` suffix. Two examples follow:

Searching Globally

The `getElementsByTagNameNS()`method (shown in Listing 6.26) is provided for searching the descendants of either an element or document object.

```
Document.getElementsByTagNameNS(String namespace,
    String localName)
Element.getElementsByTagNameNS(String namespace,
    String localName)
```

Listing 6.26 The getElementsByTagNameNS() methods

The "*" character can be used as the value for both the `namespace` and the `localName` arguments if you want a match on all namespaces or local names, respectively. For example, Listing 6.27 returns all elements with a local name of "book" regardless of the namespace.

```
NodeList nl = document.getElementsByTagNameNS("*", "book")
```

Listing 6.27 Using Document.getElementsByTagNameNS()

Working with Attributes

Attributes with namespaces are retrieved as shown in Listing 6.28.

```
// returns a String
Element.getAttributeNS(String namespaceURI, String localName)
```

Listing 6.28 The getAttributeNS() method

In Listing 6.29 below, assume `element1` is an element in an XML file having the attribute `xlink:href="www.codenotes.com"` and that the xlink prefix is mapped to the namespace `http://www.w3.org/1999/xlink`. In this circumstance, the `strAttVal` string will ultimately contain the value `www.codenotes.com`.

```
String strAttVal = element1.getAttributeNS(
    "http://www.w3.org/1999/xlink", "href");
```

Listing 6.29 Using the element.getAttributeNS() method

SUMMARY

The DOM is extremely versatile for retrieving information from an XML file. You can examine each element of the document from beginning to end or you can simply retrieve all elements with a specific tag name.

To retrieve information from a node, you can use either `Node.getName()` (to get the name of the node) or `Node.getValue()` (to get a node's content). In both methods, the return value depends on the type of node you are examining (text, attribute, element, or document).

Topic: Document Manipulation

In addition to navigation, DOM provides document manipulation methods for modifying, adding, and deleting nodes on the tree. For example, the DOM can be used to reflect a change in a clothing store's inventory XML document by updating the `quantity` attribute of a `shirt` element. You could also use the DOM to change the text content of the description element for the `shirt`.

You can use methods of the `Document` class to create new text, element, and attribute nodes. Once created, you can add attributes to elements and insert elements into the DOM document tree.

In Java, the methods presented in this section may throw a `DOMException`. The handling for `DOMException` has been excluded for brevity, but we will point out potential exception-throwing scenarios.

The same is true of Visual Basic. As errors may be raised, you should use the on error statement to trap errors. The CodeNotes website has an example of error handling in Visual Basic CN XM000681.

CONCEPTS

Adding a New Attribute

The `Element.setAttribute()` method is used to add or update an attribute to an element in a DOM tree. To add or update an attribute, pass in the attribute name and the attribute value as shown in Listing 6.30.

```
//book is a valid element object
book.setAttribute("read", "no");
```

Listing 6.30 Creating an attribute (the short way)

The `book.setAttribute` code fragment in Listing 6.30 adds an attribute to `book` with the name `"read"` and will set its value to `"no"`, indicating that the book hasn't been read. Because attribute names must be unique within an element, if an attribute named `read` already exists for the `book` element, then its value will simply be updated to "`no`". A new attribute will not be created.

Attempting to add an attribute with an invalid name throws an exception. See the Attributes section in Chapter 3 for the rules regarding attribute names.

The `Document.createAttribute()`, `Attr.setValue()`, and `Element.setAttributeNode()` methods can also be used to create an attribute. The code fragment in Listing 6.31 is functionally equivalent to that in Listing 6.30.

```
//doc is a valid document, book is a valid element
//create attribute node on the DOC and use
Attr newAttr = doc.createAttribute("read");
newAttr.setValue("no");
book.setAttributeNode(newAttr);
```

Listing 6.31 Creating an attribute (the long way)

You can use the `setValue()` method to change the value of a node you have selected using any of the navigation methods discussed in the last topic.

Getting a Document object

The node creation methods are tied to the `Document` object. In order to create a new element or text node, you must first call `document.createTextNode(String value)` or `document.createElement(String name)`.

When you create the node, it is not automatically appended to the document. Instead, it remains separate from the document until you use the other manipulation methods to insert the node into a specific location within the tree.

As you will see later in this topic, the two-step nature of building a node (and then assigning it to a location) can create some interesting problems. For example, you can easily try to add a node to itself. Fortunately, most DOM parsers will catch these "paradox" errors and either throw an exception (in Java) or raise an error event (in VB).

You can obtain a particular node's document object at any time by calling the `getOwnerDocument()` method on any valid node. Listing 6.32 demonstrates how you can obtain the document object from any node.

```
// anyNode is any Node object - Element, Attr, or Text
Document owner = anyNode.getOwnerDocument()
```

Listing 6.32 Retrieving the document object

This method can be particularly useful when you need to access the document level methods to create new nodes.

Adding a New Element

You can add a new child element to a node using a combination of the `createElement()` (or `createTextNode()`) and `appendChild()` methods. Listing 6.33 creates and adds the XML fragment, "`<email>johndoe@nowhere.com</email>`" to an element named "user".

```
// doc is a DOM document, user is an existing element node
// create newElem node
Text txt = doc.createTextNode("johndoe@nowhere.com");
Element emailElement = doc.createElement("email");
//add the text to the email element
emailElement.appendChild(txt);

// add the email element to the "user" element
user.appendChild(emailElement);
```

Listing 6.33 Creating and adding an element as a child to another element

Note that before we can add the node, we have to create the text node, using `createTextNode()`. Similarly, we have to create the element node using `createElement()`. Unlike the text node, the element node requires a name ("email" in this case). Remember, when you create a new text or element node, it is not automatically attached to the document, you must explicitly insert into the document.

Once you have built the elements, you need to arrange the order by placing the text node (email address) under the element node (`<email>` tag). In this case, we use `appendChild()` to put the text node at the end of list of child elements in the `emailElement` node. Similarly, we use the same method to move the `emailElement` node (and its children) to the end of the `user` element.

The process of moving the node to its new location is further explained in the next section.

Moving an Element

Once you have created a new node (or found a node you want to move), you have two choices for assigning it to a particular point in the DOM tree. The first method, `appendChild()`, requires that you have a reference to the new parent node. The second method, `insertBefore()`, requires that you have a reference to the parent and the next sibling node. Both methods are explained below:

appendChild()

The `appendChild()` method may be used to append a node (and all of its children) to a new parent. Simply call the `appendChild()` method on the new parent, and pass in the node you want to attach. This method was illustrated in Listing 6.33. First, we appended the text node to the `emailElement` node. Then we appended `emailElement` to the `user` node.

The `appendChild()` method actually disconnects the new node from its current parent and reattaches it to the new parent (used to call the method). The new node is always placed last in the new parent's list of child elements. This means you can always use `appendChild()`, even if the new parent does not currently have any children.

This method can, however, throw exceptions if you try to create a paradox, such as appending a node to itself. Similarly, if you are trying to move a node, you cannot append it to one of its own descendants. Again, this would create a paradox; the node tree would have a circular reference. This pattern holds true for all of the DOM node manipulation methods. If you try to create a paradox, the parser will report an error.

insertBefore()

The `appendChild()` method will always add the new node as the last child element of the new parent. The `insertBefore()` method, on the other hand, will insert the new node in any position in the list of child elements. For example, if you had a series of nodes: A, B, C, D, you could insert a new node (node Z) anywhere in the sequence, including at the end of the list.

The `insertBefore()` method works with both the parent and the next sibling in the list of child nodes. In the earlier example, if we wanted to insert node Z between nodes B and C, we would need a reference to the parent node and node C. We would then call the `insertBefore()` method on the parent and pass in both the reference to node C and the reference to node Z. This method is illustrated in Listing 6.34:

```
parentNode.insertBefore(newNode, nextSiblingNode);
```

Listing 6.34 Using insertBefore()

If you want to add the new node to the end of the list, pass in `null` as the second argument of the `insertBefore()` method.

Much like `appendChild()`, `insertBefore()` will throw an exception if you try to create a paradox. These exceptions typically occur when the nextSiblingNode is not actually a child of the parentNode. Another common paradox occurs when the newNode is already an ancestor of the parentNode (circular reference).

Copying a Node

Where insertBefore() and appendChild() move an element to a new location on the tree without copying (essentially cut and paste), the cloneNode() method actually duplicates an existing node. You can use cloneNode() in combination with insertBefore() or appendChild() to copy node instances. In Listing 6.35, the first child of element1 is copied and placed at the end of the NodeList for element2.

```
// element1 and element2 are valid node objects
Node nodeToCopy = element1.getFirstChild()
Node copyOfNode = nodeToCopy.cloneNode(true);
element2.appendChild(copyOfNode);
```

Listing 6.35 The cloneNode() method

The cloneNode() method requires a boolean parameter indicating whether the node's descendants should be copied. When the boolean value is true (as in Listing 6.36, below), nodeToCopy's attributes (if it is an Element), and all of nodeToCopy's descendant nodes will be copied (a deep copy). Otherwise, only nodeToCopy and its attributes will be copied; any descendants will be ignored (a shallow copy).

Unlike the earlier methods, it is very difficult to create a paradox by copying a node. In other words, cloneNode() will almost never throw an exception.

Removing a Node

The removeChild() method removes a node (and therefore all its descendants) from a tree. Simply call the removeChild() method from the parent, and pass in a reference to the child node that should be removed. In Listing 6.36 the first child of parentNode is removed:

```
// parentNode is a node, with at least one child node
Node nodeToRemove = parentNode.getFirstChild();
parentNode.removeChild(nodeToRemove);
```

Listing 6.36 The removeChild method

You can use this method to remove any node except the DOM document (which doesn't have a parent). Note that removeChild() throws an exception if the "removed" node (`nodeToRemove`) is not a child of the object (`parentNode`).

Replacing a node

While you can modify an existing node by changing its value and attributes, it is often more efficient to simply replace the existing node with a new node. The `replaceChild()` method can be used to replace an existing node (and its descendants) with a new node (and the new node's descendants). The `replaceChild()` method is very convenient for rearranging an XML document. Listing 6.37 replaces the first child in `parentNode` with `newNode`.

```
// parentNode is a node with at least one child
// newNode is an unattached node
Node oldNode = parentNode.getFirstChild();
parentNode.replaceChild(newNode, oldNode);
```

Listing 6.37 Replacing a node

Once again, you have to be careful not to create paradox situations. The `replaceChild()` method throws an exception if the replaced node (`oldNode`) is not a child of the calling node (`parentNode`). It will also throw an exception if you attempt to use an ancestor (of `parentNode`) as the replacement node (circular reference again).

EXAMPLE

Modifying the Contents of a Neighborhood Library's Inventory

In this example, we will start with an XML document outlining books as they might appear in a neighborhood library's card catalogue (Listing 6.38).

```
<?xml version="1.0"?>
<library>
<book isbn="7423598534">
  <author><fname>Orson</fname><lname>Card</lname></author>
  <title>Ender&apos;s Game</title>
</book>
<!-- &apos; is the entity for creating an apostrophe -->
<!-- additional books removed for brevity -->
</library>
```

Listing 6.38 library.xml

Using the methods outlined in this topic, we will modify the `library.xml` file by adding a new attribute `available` and a new child element (`<genre>`) to the book element. The resulting XML will look like Listing 6.39 (bolded text indicates the changes):

```
<library>
<book isbn="7423598534" available="YES">
  <author><fname>Orson</fname><lname>Card</lname></author>
  <title>Ender&apos;s Game</title>
  <genre>Science Fiction</genre>
</book>

</library>
```

Listing 6.39 The modified library.xml

For brevity, the process of selecting a particular book element has been omitted. However, this process is similar to the example "Retrieving the Price of a Stock from an XML File" in the Document Navigation topic earlier in this chapter.

The `addInfo()` method (Listing 6.40) will update each book node by adding the attribute and genre nodes:

```
private static void addInfo(Element book) {
  // needed for the createXXXX() methods
  Document doc = book.getOwnerDocument();
  // add attribute
  book.setAttribute("available", "YES");
  // add element and text
  Element genre = doc.createElement("genre");
  Text sciFi = doc.createTextNode("Science Fiction");
  genre.appendChild(sciFi);
  book.appendChild(genre);
}
```

Listing 6.40 Source code for the addInfo method

Saving a modified file is different for each implementation of the DOM. Both the MSXML3 and JAXP versions are discussed under How and Why, below.

HOW AND WHY

How Do I Rename an Element or Attribute?

The DOM doesn't support renaming of elements or attributes. Only the value of an element or attribute may be changed, and not its name. In order to rename an element or attribute, you should remove the old element or attribute and add a new one.

Can a Validated Document Be Made Invalid Using the DOM?

Yes. For example, you could add a new element to an XML document that is not specified in that document's DTD. There is nothing in the DOM to prevent you from invalidating a document.

How Do I Save a Modified Document?

Surprisingly, the DOM Level 2 standard does not provide any standard method for writing to a file, though most implementations provide (non-standard) support.

JAXP provides `Node.toString()`, which returns a node and its children as an XML string. The code in Listing 6.41 copies `library.xml` to `libraryCopy.xml` (using the `java.io` package).

```
//assumes import of java.io.* and org.w3c.dom.*
// parse the document
DocumentBuilder builder;
DocumentBuilderFactory factory =
DocumentBuilderFactory.newInstance();
builder = factory.newDocumentBuilder();
Document document = builder.parse("file:library.xml");
Element root = document.getDocumentElement();
String strXML = root.toString();

// write to the file
File outputFile = new File("libraryCopy.xml");
FileWriter out = new FileWriter(outputFile);
out.write(strXML);
out.close();
```

Listing 6.41 Saving an XML file to disk using JAXP

In MSXML3, the `IXMLDomNode.xml` property acts as a `toString()` method. The code to save an XML file to disk when using MSXML3 is shown in Listing 6.42 (this fragment requires adding a reference to the Microsoft Scripting Runtime library):

```
Dim fso As New FileSystemObject
Dim txt As TextStream
Dim doc As New DOMDocument
Dim display As IXMLDOMNode
Dim strXML As String

' load and parse the XML document
doc.Load "file:c:\temp\library.xml"
Set display = doc.documentElement
strXML = display.xml

' write and close the new file
Set txt = fso.CreateTextFile("c:\temp\libraryCopy.xml")
txt.Write strXML
txt.Close
```

Listing 6.42 Saving an XML file to disk using MSXML3 (using VB)

DOM Level 3, when released, will likely provide standardized support for creating XML files.

How Do I Work with Namespaces When Manipulating Nodes?

The DOM methods for working with namespaces are quite similar to those without namespaces. All methods for working with namespaces have the suffix `NS` and act the same as the corresponding method that operates without `NS`. The namespace arguments accept an additional `string` parameter, which is the name of the namespace.

Adding Attributes

As with adding attributes that do not have namespaces, there are two ways in which to add attributes to an element with a namespace.

The first method looks like this:

```
Element.setAttributeNS(String namespaceURI,
    String qualifiedName, String value);
```

The second method looks like this:

```
Document.createAttributeNS(String namespaceURI,
    String qualifiedName);
AttrFromAbove.setValue(String value);
Element.setAttributeNodeNS(AttrFromAbove);
```

To add the attribute `xlink:href="www.CodeNotes.com"` to `elem` where `xlink` maps to the namespace URI `http://www.w3.org/1999/xlink`, use the code in Listing 6.43.

```
elem.setAttributeNS("http://www.w3.org/1999/xlink",
    "xlink:href", "www.CodeNotes.com");
```

Listing 6.43 Adding an attribute with a namespace

Adding Elements

The `Document.CreateElementNS()` method (Listing 6.44) is used to create an element with a given namespace and qualified name. Once you have created the element, you can add it to the document using any of the methods discussed previously (`appendChild()`, `insertChild()`, or `replaceChild()`).

```
Document.createElementNS(String namespaceURI,
    String qualifiedName);
```

Listing 6.44 The Document.createElementNS() method

SUMMARY

The DOM allows you to modify the contents of an XML file in any way you wish. Elements, attributes, and text can be moved around within the document, created and added to the document, or removed entirely from the document. It is also possible to copy a node and place the copy in another part of the document.

Chapter Summary

DOM is a workhorse API designed for manipulation of XML documents. DOM provides a complete, random-access view of the elements, attributes, and text in an XML document, and has full support for modifying the tree. Common extensions provided by most implementations include XPath support and saving documents to disk.

The DOM API is especially appropriate for document-oriented processing, such as maintaining a document in memory for some time while the user works on the data.

However, the DOM API can be very slow when parsing large documents and may not be appropriate if you require only specific elements out of the XML document. The Simple API for XML (SAX) model provides an alternative solution for these circumstances, as you will see in the next chapter.

Chapter 7

PROGRAMMING WITH SAX

The Simple API for XML (SAX) is a read-only event-driven parser interface developed by David Megginson, a former member of the W3C. Unlike the other technologies presented in this CodeNote, SAX was created independently of the W3C, but its simplicity and efficiency have made it a popular ad-hoc standard. The best starting point for SAX support is http://www.megginson.com/SAX.

SAX is an *event-based* API, which means that it reports results back to the application (or "calls back") as the XML file is parsed. Conceptually, SAX parsers break an XML file into pieces, notifying your application after each piece has been parsed with messages like "encountered an element start-tag" or "encountered some text." This differs from the DOM, which parses an XML file completely and then presents your application with a complete node tree. SAX gives your application the opportunity to store only the information it needs as the parse progresses and to discard the rest.

This chapter explains when and how to use SAX to process an XML document. This CodeNote covers SAX 2.0, which includes support for namespaces and validation, and in which a significant number of SAX 1.0 classes and methods have been deprecated or renamed.

SIMPLE APPLICATION

This chapter presents two simple applications, one in Java and one in Visual Basic (with COM). Both applications perform similar functions.

SAX Parsing Using Java

The following example parses an XML document (`hello.xml`) and displays the content on the screen as text. As the SAX parser reads the document, it issues calls back to the program (or launches events) every time it encounters something interesting, such as an XML tag. The program then traps the events and performs an action (such as writing the tag contents to the screen).

The example consists of three parts: a handler class to trap the events SAX will call as it parses the document (`Handler.java`), a main program (`Sample.java`) that will house the handler and "kick off" the parsing, and a sample XML file (`hello.xml`).

The Java-based example programs in this chapter require the installation of Sun's JAXP 1.1 as outlined in Chapter 2. Also, be certain that your `CLASSPATH` variable points to `jaxp.jar` and `crimson.jar`.

```
import org.xml.sax.*;
import org.xml.sax.helpers.*;

class Handler extends DefaultHandler {
  // SAX calls this method when it encounters an element
  public void startElement(String strNamespaceURI,
      String strLocalName, String strQName, Attributes al)
      throws SAXException{
    System.out.println("startElement: " + strLocalName);
  }

  /* SAX calls this method to pass in character data
  stored between the start and end tags of a particular
  element */
  public void characters(char[] a, int s, int l)
      throws SAXException{
    System.out.println("characters: " + new String(a, s, l));
  }

  /* SAX calls this method when the end-tag for an
  element is encountered */
  public void endElement(String strNamespaceURI,
      String strLocalName, String strQName)
```

```
        throws SAXException{
      System.out.println("endElement: /" + strLocalName);
    }
}
```

Listing 7.1 Handler.java

Note that the handler class (`Handler.java`) traps three events: the start of a tag, character data, and the end of a tag. The tag events (`startElement()` and `endElement()`) will print the name of the tag to the screen, while the `characters()` event will print the tag content to the screen.

The next program, `Sample.java`, creates a new instance of the handler class, a SAX parser, and starts the parsing of an XML file named `hello.xml`.

```
import org.xml.sax.*;
import org.xml.sax.helpers.*;
import javax.xml.parsers.*;

public class Sample {
  public static void main(String[] args) throws Exception {
    // create a handler
    Handler handler = new Handler();
    // create a parser
    SAXParserFactory spf = SAXParserFactory.newInstance();
    XMLReader parser = null;
    SAXParser saxParser = spf.newSAXParser();
    parser = saxParser.getXMLReader();
    // assign the handler to the parser
    parser.setContentHandler (handler);
    // parse the document
    parser.parse("hello.xml");
  }
}
```

Listing 7.2 Sample.java

Save and compile both Java files. Using any text editor, create an XML file named `hello.xml` with the following content:

```
<?xml version="1.0"?>
<name>Teresa Valentino</name>
```

Listing 7.3 hello.xml

Make sure that the XML file and both compiled class files (`Handler.class` and `Sample.class`) are in the same directory and start the program with: `java Sample`. The output will look like this:

```
startElement: name
characters: Teresa Valentino
endElement: /name
```

SAX Parsing Using Visual Basic/COM

In the previous section, we parsed an XML file, `hello.xml`, using the Sun JAXP version of SAX. The example in this section will use Visual Basic in conjunction with Microsoft's MSXML parser. Specifically, it will parse the XML document `hello.xml` and output the content to a VB text box. The output in the text box will look identical to that produced by the Java example.

The example consists of two parts: a form to implement a handler and parse the document (`Sample.frm`), and a handler class to handle events (`Handler.cls`). In order for this example to work, you must install MSXML as outlined in Chapter 2. You must then create a new Visual Basic project and add a reference (via the Project | References dialog) to MSXML30. The MSXML30 type library will be listed in this dialog as `Microsoft XML v3.0`. Make sure this entry is checked. The first section of code builds the handler object (`Handler.cls`), and the second section uses the handler in the `Form_Load()` method of the application.

In your project, create a new class module named `Handler`:

```
Implements IVBSAXContentHandler
Dim myTB As TextBox

Public Sub SetTextBox(myTextBox As TextBox)
  Set myTB = myTextBox
End Sub

' this method outputs the element start-tag
Private Sub IVBSAXContentHandler_startElement _
  (strNamespaceURI As String, strLocalName As String, _
  strQName As String, ByVal oAttributes As _
  MSXML2.IVBSAXAttributes)

  myTB.text = myTB.text & "startElement: " _
      & strLocalName & VbCrLf
End Sub
```

```
' this method outputs the elements character data
Private Sub IVBSAXContentHandler_characters _
    (strChars As String)

  myTB.text = myTB.text & "characters: " _
      & strChars & VbCrLf
End Sub

' this method outputs the element end-tag
Private Sub IVBSAXContentHandler_endElement( _
  strNamespaceURI As String, strLocalName As String, _
  strQName As String)

  myTB.text = myTB.text & "endElement: /" & strLocalName _
  & VbCrLf
End Sub

'Because Handler implements IVBSAXContentHandler, we have
'to add definitions for the following :
Private Property Set _
    IVBSAXContentHandler_documentLocator(ByVal _
  RHS As MSXML2.IVBSAXLocator)
End Property
Private Sub IVBSAXContentHandler_startDocument()
End Sub
Private Sub IVBSAXContentHandler_endDocument()
End Sub
Private Sub IVBSAXContentHandler_startPrefixMapping( _
    strPrefix As String, strURI As String)
End Sub
Private Sub IVBSAXContentHandler_endPrefixMapping(_
    strPrefix As String)
End Sub
Private Sub IVBSAXContentHandler_ignorableWhitespace( _
    strChars As String)
End Sub
Private Sub IVBSAXContentHandler_processingInstruction( _
    strTarget As String, strData As String)
End Sub
Private Sub IVBSAXContentHandler_skippedEntity( _
  strName As String)
End Sub
```

Listing 7.4   Handler.cls

Much like the Java example, Handler.cls implements methods that respond to start-tags (`*_startElement()`), end-tags (`*_endElement()`), and character content (`*_endElement()`). Unlike in Java, you are required to implement the full set of methods, even if you do not intend to use them. Therefore, you have empty methods for the other events (e.g., `*_endDocument()`, `*_documentLocater()`, etc.).

Once you have built the handler class, add a text box to your form named `txtMyBox`. Remove the default text and set the MultiLine property to true. Then, add the following code to the `Form_Load()` method. This code will execute when you start the program:

```
Private Sub Form_Load()
  ' create a handler and a parser
  Dim handler As clsHandler
  Dim myXML As SAXXMLReader

  Set handler = New clsHandler
  Set myXML = New SAXXMLReader

  ' assign a textbox as the output destination
  handler.SetTextBox txtMyBox

  ' assign the handler to the parser
  Set myXML.contentHandler = handler

  ' parse the document
  myXML.parseURL ("file:hello.xml")
End Sub
```

Listing 7.5 Sample.frm

This code will create the handler and the parser, load the document, and display the results in the text box. Before you run the program, be sure to create the `hello.xml` file as shown in Listing 7.3 in the Java example. Put the file in the same directory as your VB program. When you run the program, the text box should show:

```
startElement: name
characters: Teresa Valentino
endElement: /name
```

CORE CONCEPTS

SAX Is Event Driven

SAX allows the extraction of information from an XML document without the overhead of loading it entirely into memory. SAX is therefore particularly suited to performing one-pass processing on large XML documents, perhaps searching for specific items or finding totals.

SAX operates by reading a small fragment of the XML (e.g., an opening tag), and making a *callback* into your application, telling your application, "I have encountered a tag." It then reads another fragment, makes another callback, and so on. SAX itself maintains practically no state information, and your application maintains only what it needs to accomplish the task at hand.

For example, if you were totaling the number of elements in an XML document, your program would need only to maintain a single numerical value. You would not need to maintain names or contents of elements and attributes.

Consider parsing an XML document using:

```
System.out.println("Start");
parser.parse("person.xml");
Systtem.out.println("End");
```

Listing 7.6 Parsing an XML document

Figure 7.1 illustrates what actually happens.

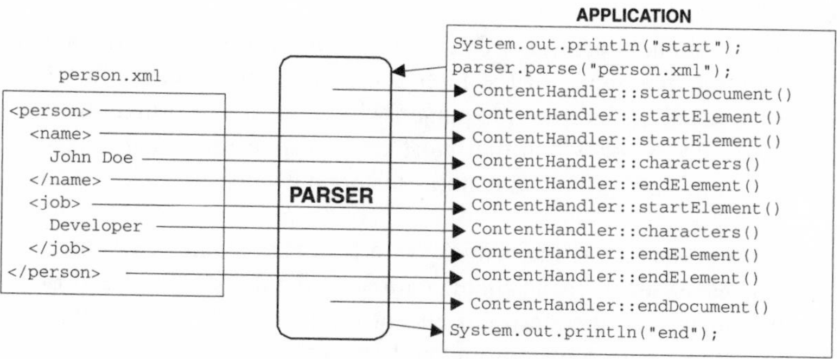

Figure 7.1 The SAX parse() method reads XML fragments and makes many callbacks back into the application, before finally returning control to the application.

SAX Parsers

Many parsers implement the SAX API (and, in fact, most DOM parsers are built on top of SAX parsers).

This chapter explicitly illustrates the use of several Java parsers, including the default JAXP 1.1 SAX parser, Crimson. Crimson was originally developed by Sun and is now maintained by the Apache Software Foundation (http://www.apache.org).

Should the performance, stability, or compliance of Crimson prove inadequate, two very good, freely available open source alternatives are:

- **XML4J** (http://www.alphaworks.ibm.com/tech/xml4j) is IBM's open source XML parser for Java. The SAX2 driver for XML4J is packaged under `com.ibm.xml.parser.SAXParser`.
- **Xerces Java Parser** (http://xml.apache.org/xerces-j/), maintained by the Apache Foundation, shares much of its codebase with XML4J. XML4J includes a native SAX2 driver located in the package: `org.apache.xerces.parsers.SAXParser`. Be sure to add the `xerces.jar` file to your `CLASSPATH` environment variable to access Xerces.

This chapter also discusses Microsoft's XML parser, MSXML, which you will need if you want to use SAX with Visual Basic. Significant differences between the Java and Visual Basic implementations will be pointed out throughout the chapter.

Installation procedures for both JAXP and MSXML can be found in Chapter 2 (Installation).

SAX Interfaces

The SAX callbacks are defined in four interfaces. You must write a handler to implement each of the interfaces. Each implemented interface will receive callbacks from the parser, which include information about the XML pieces for which the interface is responsible. Each interface performs different tasks and handles different events:

- `ContentHandler` is the primary interface for parsing XML files. `ContentHandler` encapsulates callbacks for the start and end of the document, the start and end of elements, and for character text stored between start- and end-tags of an element.
- `ErrorHandler` allows you to customize handling for fatal and nonfatal parsing errors, as well as warnings.
- `DTDHandler` receives information about the Document Type Definition (DTD). Document type definitions were discussed in Chapter 3.

- `EntityResolver` allows your application to intercept requests from the parser for external entities. A callback would be triggered, for example, to resolve a URL for an external DTD. External entities are discussed in Document Type Definitions in Chapter 3.

When starting out with SAX, the `DTDHandler` and `EntityResolver` interfaces are rarely used, as their functionalities are extremely limited and are not often required. We'll focus on the `ContentHandler` and `ErrorHandler` interfaces.

Topic: Introduction to SAX

Parsing an XML document with SAX involves two basic blocks of code. The first is the *handler* class, in which you must implement each of the four interfaces discussed in the SAX Interfaces section above. The second involves creating and instantiating a parser object in your application, instantiating your handler object, and passing the handler to the parser. The parser object will translate the XML document and call events in your handler class.

CONCEPTS

Creating a Handler Class

When parsing an XML document, the SAX parser will execute the appropriate callback methods on your handler class, depending upon what type of information it encounters. For example, you can instruct the handler to perform certain tasks when the parser reaches the beginning of an element, or when it encounters character data.

One approach to creating a handler class is to implement all four SAX interfaces directly, as shown in Listing 7.7.

```
import org.xml.sax.*;

public class myHandler implements ContentHandler,
  ErrorHandler, DTDHandler, EntityResolver {}
```

Listing 7.7 Implementing the four SAX interfaces

Obviously, implementing an interface means that one must provide implementations for all the methods of that interface. Often, a SAX developer will write one or more "empty" methods consisting of nothing more than an open and close brace for those callback methods in which he or she is not interested.

There is, however, a better way: using the `DefaultHandler` *adapter* class. Adapter classes implement interfaces with empty-method bodies so that classes derived from them don't have to implement all of the methods. `DefaultHandler` implements empty-method bodies for all of the methods in `ContentHandler`, `ErrorHandler`, `DTDHandler`, and `EntityResolver`. Your handler class can extend `DefaultHandler`, which means it needs to override only the methods you wish to be called. For example, if you wanted to process only element start-tags, you would need to implement only one method in your handler (`startElement()`), instead of all of them. Listing 7.8 shows an example class that extends `DefaultHandler()` and implements no methods.

```
import org.xml.sax.*;
import org.xml.sax.helpers.*;

public class myHandler extends DefaultHandler {}
```

Listing 7.8 Extending DefaultHandler

Unfortunately, Visual Basic does not have an adapter class, and you must explicitly implement each interface. This often means you have to create many empty functions. However, with the Visual Basic Development Environment, implementing the empty methods is trivial.

ContentHandler Methods

The `ContentHandler` interface is, perhaps, the most important SAX interface you can implement. The parser calls the `ContentHandler` methods as it moves through an XML document and encounters different XML elements. The `ContentHandler` interface has eleven methods, each of which operates on a particular type of data received from the parser. For example, the handler's `startElement()` method is called whenever the parser finds an element start-tag. If your handler extends the `DefaultHandler` helper class, you need only implement the methods you wish to override, and leave out the rest. The five most commonly used `ContentHandler` methods are described below:

startDocument()

The `startDocument()` method is called exactly once for each document, when parsing first commences.

```
public void startDocument() {}
```

Bear in mind that your handler may be used to parse multiple documents; thus, totals, flags, and other variables should be initialized in this method and not in the constructor of your handler.

endDocument()
The `endDocument()` method is called at the end of a document, when there is no more data to process. You might, for example, use this method to output totals or statistics for the document, or clean up any open resources.

```
public void endDocument() {}
```

Like `startDocument()`, `endDocument()` is simply a notification method and has no arguments.

startElement()
The `startElement()` method is called whenever the parser encounters an element start-tag, such as `<person>`, `<book>`, `<movie>`, or any other tag that does not begin with a `/`. The `startElement()` callback receives four parameters from the parser:

1. The element's namespace URI, e.g., `http://www.mynamespace.org`. If the element is not part of a namespace, the URI will be an empty string.
2. The element's local name, e.g., `person`.
3. The element's qualified name, e.g., `ns:person`. If the element is not part of a namespace, the qualified name and the local name will be identical.
4. A list of the element's attributes as an `Attributes` object, which will be discussed in the next section, Attributes.

```
public void startElement(String namespaceURI,
  String localName, String qualifiedName, Attributes attList) {}
```

endElement()
The `endElement()` method is called whenever the parser encounters an element end-tag, such as `</element>`. The parameters are the same as `startElement()`, except that `endElement()` does not receive the attribute list.

```
public void endElement(String namespaceURI,
  String localName, String qualifiedName) {}
```

characters()

The `characters()` method is called whenever the parser encounters text within an element. This method receives a byte array along with the offset (more on this in a moment) and length of the data.

```
public void characters(char[] text, int start, int length) {}
```

Depending on the SAX parser and size of the character element, the parser may call the `characters()` callback many times for a single text block. If this happens, the start variable acts as an indicator of the current position within the character stream. When parsing character callbacks, you should append the character array to a `StringBuffer` in Java, or a string data type in Visual Basic, and examine the contents only within the `endElement()` callback. We'll see an example of this later in this topic.

Other ContentHandler Methods

The six other `ContentHandler` methods are not necessary in most situations. These include methods for processing whitespace, processing instructions, and skipped external entities. Example code leveraging each of these methods is available on the CodeNotes website CN XM000702.

Attributes

Attributes are passed into your handler when the parser calls `startElement()`. The fourth parameter of `startElement()` is an `Attributes` object reference. The `Attributes` interface contains methods for extracting attribute names and values from an XML start-tag.

The `Attributes.getLength()` method allows you to determine the number of attributes in an element start-tag. This is useful if you want to iterate through all the attributes for an element.

```
int numAtts = attList.getLength();
```

Attributes are assigned index numbers by the parser. Using these index numbers, you can access the attributes' characteristics. Listing 7.9 shows sample code for accessing various attribute characteristics:

```
//Assumes attList is a valid AttributeList object
// Find an attribute's local name by index number
String attname = attList.getLocalName(index);

// Find an attribute's namespace URI by index number
String attURI = attList.getURI(index);

// Find an attribute's qualified name by index number
String attQname = attList.getQName(index);

// Find an attribute's value by index number
String attValue = attList.getValue(index);
```

Listing 7.9 Accessing attribute characteristics

You can also retrieve an attribute's value by providing a namespace URI and local name, or a qualified name, as shown in Listing 7.10.

```
String attValue = attList.getValue(attURI, attname);
String attValue = attList.getValue(attQname);
```

Listing 7.10 Retrieving attribute values by attribute name

Two important notes on the `Attributes` interface:

1. Attributes are assigned arbitrary index numbers by the parser. These numbers are *not related* to the order in which the attributes appear in the XML document. Also note that Attribute indexes are 0-based.
2. The interface reference for an attribute is valid *only* during the `startElement()` call. If you wish to persist attribute information beyond this, you may do so by instantiating an `AttributesImpl` object. This object allows you to take a persistent snapshot of an `Attributes` reference.

```
attImpl = new AttributesImpl(attList);
```

Within a callback, you will need to save these objects in a list, tree, or some other data member of your handler class.

Creating the SAX Parser

Once you have created your handler class and implemented its methods, you need to create an instance of a SAX parser and supply it with your handler as a parameter.

Creating a Handler Instance

The handler receives all the events encountered by the parser and perform actions on data according to how you have configured its methods.

```
// Assumes you have created a handler class
// called "Handler"
Handler h = new Handler();
```

Listing 7.11 Creating a handler instance

Creating an XMLReader Instance

`XMLReader` is the SAX2 term for an XML parser. The `XMLReader` interface contains the methods used to parse the document. There are several ways in which to create an instance of `XMLReader`.

1. ***Using JAXP***. JAXP provides a class called `SAXParser`, which can be used to create an instance of `XMLReader`. Generally, when you instantiate `XMLReader`, you have to specify the location of the SAX parser (sometimes called a `driver`) that you are using. JAXP instantiates `XMLReader` with its default SAX driver, Crimson, so that you don't have to specify one. In order for the code in Listing 7.12 to work, you must have installed JAXP 1.1 as detailed in Chapter 2.

```
// use SAXParserFactory to create a new JAXP SAXParser
SAXParserFactory spf = SAXParserFactory.newInstance();
SAXParser saxParser = spf.newSAXParser();

// use JAXP SAXParser to get a SAX XMLReader instance
XMLReader parser = saxParser.getXMLReader();
```

Listing 7.12 Creating an XMLReader instance with JAXP

2. ***Using Another Parser***. To use a parser other than JAXP's default parser (Crimson) you will need to use an `XMLReaderFactory` to create an instance of `XMLReader`. `XMLReaderFactory` has a method named `createXMLReader()` that accepts a fully qualified name of a SAX driver. Listing 7.13 shows the creation of an `XMLReader` instance using the Xerces parser.

```
XMLReader parser = XMLReaderFactory.createXMLReader
    ("org.apache.xerces.parsers.SAXParser");
```

Listing 7.13 Creating an XMLReader instance with an alternate parser

3. ***Setting the System Property***. You can change the default driver by adding a system property called `org.xml.sax.driver`, with the name of the desired parser. For example, if you were using the Xerces parser, the value of the `org.xml.sax.driver` system property would be `"org.apache.xerces.parsers.SAXParser"`. `XMLReaderFactory.createXMLReader()` can then be called without any parameters. This option allows your code to be parser-independent, although the program will fail at run time if the system property has not been set.

Parsing the Document

Finally, you must assign your handler to the `XMLReader` instance and parse the document, as shown in Listing 7.14:

```
// setContentHandler() method assigns the handler you
// created to the XMLReader instance
parser.setContentHandler (handler);
// parse() method commences parsing the XML
parser.parse("document.xml");
```

Listing 7.14 Assigning a handler to the XMLReader and parsing a document

SAX with MSXML3 and Visual Basic

The SAX2 standard is specified as a set of Java classes and interfaces. These have been faithfully adopted by Microsoft in MSXML3 as a set of COM interfaces and objects.

The essential part of an application that leverages SAX involves the SAX parser calling back to a handler class that implements the methods of `ContentHandler`. In Visual Basic, the `ContentHandler` interface is named `IVBSAXContentHandler`. To create a handler in Visual Basic, we need to write a VB Class that implements the `IVBSAXContentHandler` interface:

```
Implements IVBSAXContentHandler
```

The `Implements` keyword is used to specify that a given Visual Basic class will provide an implementation of an interface.

The implementing methods must be named in the form *`interface_method`*. For example, the following method declaration is for the `startDocument()` method in `IVBSAXContentHandler`:

```
Public Sub IVBSAXContentHandler_startDocument()
  ' implementation
End Sub
```

The MSXML3 implementation is quite faithful to the original specification. `IVBSAXContentHandler`, for example, defines almost identical methods to those in Java's `ContentHandler`.

The remaining code in this chapter is presented in Java, though the concepts and code constructs are essentially the same for MSXML3.

One difference to note between MSXML and JAXP is that the MSXML3 SAX implementation does *not* support validation. That is, MSXML3 does not allow you to validate your XML documents against a DTD or schema (discussed in Chapter 8) during parsing.

EXAMPLES

Once again, the following examples are in Java. The Visual Basic equivalents are fairly similar with the caveats mentioned in the previous section. Visual Basic source code is available on the CodeNotes website (use the pointers at the end of each example).

General XML Traversal

The first example illustrates a general handler class that outputs element names and text for a given XML file. In Listing 7.15, the `main()` method instantiates the parser, creates the handler instance (an instance of `myHandler`), and parses the document.

Normally, you would want a separate class to instantiate the handler and the parser and to begin the parsing process (as illustrated in Listing 7.1 and 7.2, earlier in the chapter). In the interest of brevity, we have combined the two classes:

```
import org.xml.sax.*;
import org.xml.sax.helpers.*;
import javax.xml.parsers.*;

public class myHandler extends DefaultHandler {
  // Create a buffer to hold characters() data
  private StringBuffer buffer = new StringBuffer();

  // Create handler and XMLReader instances and parse XML
  public static void main(String[] args) {
    try {
      myHandler handler = new myHandler();
      SAXParserFactory spf = SAXParserFactory.newInstance();
      SAXParser saxParser = spf.newSAXParser();
```

```
      XMLReader parser = saxParser.getXMLReader();
      parser.setContentHandler (handler);
      parser.parse ("document.xml");
    } catch(Exception e) {}
  }

  // Print out element names
  public void startElement(String namespaceURI,
      String localName, String qualifiedName,
      Attributes attList) throws SAXException {
    System.out.print(localName + ": ");
  }

  // Append character data to buffer
  public void characters(char[] text, int start,
      int length) throws SAXException {
    buffer.append(text,start,length);
  }

  // Output character data (trimming whitespace)
    public void endElement(String namespaceURI,
      String localName, String qualifiedName)
      throws SAXException {
    String value = (buffer.toString()).trim();
    System.out.println(value);
    //reset buffer for next element
    buffer.setLength(0);
  }
}
```

Listing 7.15 A sample SAX parse, with handler class

Assuming that our XML looks something like the following:

```
<?xml version="1.0"?>
<employees>
  <employee empid="001">
    <name>Akbar Shabazz</name>
    <position>President</position>
  </employee>
  <employee empid="002">
    <name>Eileen Dover</name>
    <position>Vice-President</position>
```

```
  </employee>
</employees>
```

Listing 7.16 document.xml

the output from the example program would look like:

```
employees: employee: name: Akbar Shabazz
position: President

employee: name: Eileen Dover
position: Vice-President
```

Listing 7.17 Output of parsing document.xml (Listing 7.16), with code from Listing 7.15

Note that the extra linebreak between the first position tag and the first employee tag is a result of using `println()` in the `endElement()` method. This `println()` statement will add a linebreak every time an end-tag is encountered. The extra linebreaks are from the "empty" end-tags, like `</employee>`.

See the CodeNotes website CN XM000782 for the complete source code in Visual Basic.

Calculating Aggregates

The next example illustrates how one can use SAX to calculate aggregates. `Counter.java` is a handler that finds the total number of elements and attributes that appear in an XML document.

```
public class counter extends DefaultHandler {
  private int elCount; //total number of elements
  private int attCount; //total number of attributes

  // Add to elcount and attcount
  public void startElement(String namespaceURI,
      String localName, String qualifiedName,
      Attributes attList) throws SAXException {
    elCount += 1;
    attCount += attList.getLength();
  }

  // Output totals in endDocument
  public void endDocument() {
```

```
        System.out.println("Total Elements: " + elcount);
        System.out.println("Total Attributes: " + attcount);
    }
}
```

Listing 7.18 Counter.java sums the elements and attributes in an XML document

The example in Listing 7.18 can easily be extended to sum values of a particular element or elements. All that is required is to place an IF THEN construct within `startElement()` to check for a certain element name, perhaps set a boolean variable to true if it is an element we are interested in, and then provide an implementation of the `characters()` method that can extract the value (if the boolean were true) and keep a running total.

HOW AND WHY

When Should I Use SAX?

You should use SAX when you need only to read an XML document and not to modify it. Also use SAX when speed and efficiency are your top priorities, as when dealing with large amounts of data in very large XML files. SAX allows you to minimize the amount of information residing in memory.

If your documents are not especially large, you might first consider DOM, due to its simplicity (no callbacks).

For many situations, such as reading a small program configuration file, either API is acceptable.

Why Shouldn't I Use the Default Crimson Parser?

When learning and experimenting with XML, it does not particularly matter which parser you use. As you progress to larger tasks, however, you may encounter performance problems, or you may wish to take advantage of the latest features (such as XML schema validation). In this circumstance you might want to explore parsers other than Crimson.

Keep in mind that the more proprietary parser functionality you take advantage of, the more difficult it will be to move your application to another parser in the future.

BUGS AND CAVEATS

Use the DefaultHandler Adapter with Care

When using adapter classes, be sure that your method signatures are correct. For example, suppose you implemented a handler method as in Listing 7.19:

```
public void StartElement(String namespaceURI,
    String localName, String qualifiedName, Attributes attList)
    throws SAXException     // Incorrect!
{
  // Code Here
}
```

Listing 7.19 Incorrect definition of a DefaultHandler method

The program would compile successfully; but the method would never be called, as you have not overridden the (null) adapter class implementation, whose function name is actually `startElement()`, with a lowercase "s," and not `StartElement()` with an uppercase "S." Always check the API documentation to make sure you are using the correct function names and signatures.

Attributes Are Unordered

The Attributes collection is ordered arbitrarily; it may or may not match the order in which the attributes appear in the XML. When you need to select a particular attribute, you should use the `getValue` methods that take URIs and local names, or qualified names, as parameters. For example, if you were parsing a fragment of XML like:

```
<car make="ford" model="taurus" color="blue">
```

and you wanted to find the model of this car, you should not use the index number to access the attribute:

```
attList.getValue(1);
```

Accessing a particular attribute by index may or may not work, because there is no guarantee that the parser will have assigned the index 1 (remember, attributes are 0-based) to the attribute `model`. Instead, you should use a `getValue()` call with a URI and local name as parameters, like this:

```
attList.getValue("","model");
```

This call should return `taurus`. Note that we provided a blank string for the URI, because we are assuming that `<car>` is not in a namespace. Namespaces in SAX are discussed in the Namespaces topic of this chapter, below.

Text May Be Passed as Multiple characters() Calls

Text blocks, even small ones, may be broken into multiple calls to `characters()`. See the `characters()` method in Listing 7.15 for an example of retrieving complete text blocks.

DESIGN NOTES

Threading Models

At first glance, it would seem as if a SAX parser is the perfect tool to use for multithreaded programming. Simply hand a section of the document to each thread and then process the results. Unfortunately, it isn't that simple, as the implementations of SAX vary from vendor to vendor.

JAXP

`SAXParser` is *not* thread-safe, so two threads may not process the same file. However, you can use one `SAXParser` instance per thread to parse multiple files simultaneously.

MSXML 3

MSXML's implementation of SAX is a COM (Component Object Model) object with a default configuration setting that makes it thread-safe.

A Note for SAX1 Developers

The original SAX1 specification did not support namespaces. SAX2 is the current standard and contains full support for namespaces, as well as additional new functionality such as selectable features (discussed later in this chapter). Many of the classes in SAX1 have been renamed or deprecated in SAX2. The class structure is the same, but the names and methods have changed to support namespaces and other new features. A list of SAX1 deprecated classes and their SAX2 equivalents or replacements can be found at `XM000701`.

Filters

A technique SAX1 developers may be familiar with is using filters, or handler objects that also generate SAX events. These objects can be chained together as an approach to code reuse. In SAX2 this approach is formalized and streamlined using the new `XMLFilter` interface. For an in-depth article on this useful technique, see the CodeNotes website CN XM000790.

SAX Alternatives

It is certainly possible to create an application that will use SAX to read an XML document, and provide its own custom code to modify the XML document as it is read. Given that SAX is read only, however, it is far simpler to use the DOM. Although, at the time of this writing, the DOM specification does not include a method for writing or modifying an XML document, most DOM implementations have the ability to do so. Thus, it can be beneficial to actually combine DOM and SAX. This combination could be useful if, for example, you wanted to parse a very large amount of XML data (something, perhaps, too large to put in memory) into a small, clean tree structure, and then write this structure into a new XML file. You could use SAX to parse the data and extract only the elements you wanted, insert them into a new DOM tree, and use DOM to write the revised XML document to a file.

SUMMARY

SAX parsers make callbacks to the application through a set of interfaces, most importantly `ContentHandler`. These interfaces are implemented by a handler class, either directly or through the use of the `DefaultHandler` adapter class. The various methods within the handler process different fragments of XML (start-tags, character data, etc.) as the parse progresses. The totals, lists, or other data structures that your application builds during these callbacks become the end result of your processing.

Topic: Stack-Based Processing

When parsing with SAX, you are essentially performing a depth-first traversal over a tree. Because SAX does not maintain state information, finding information about an element's ancestors can complicate matters. Very often, in order to do nontrivial processing, you will want to maintain a structure of the current element's ancestors, up to the root. The best way to maintain this information is in a stack, pushing elements on the stack in `startElement()` and popping elements off the stack in `endElement()`.

For example, suppose you were using SAX to parse an XML document with recursive elements, arranged as in Listing 7.20:

```
<?xml version="1.0"?>
<lifeguards>
  <lifeguard empid="001">
    <name>Jane Jones</name>
    <position>Head Lifeguard</position>
    <lifeguard>
      <name>Fred Smith</name>
      <position>Senior Lifeguard</position>
      <lifeguard>
        <name>Sally Johnson</name>
        <position>Junior Lifeguard</position>
      </lifeguard>
      <lifeguard>
        <name>Joe Williams</name>
        <position>Junior Lifeguard</position>
      </lifeguard>
    </lifeguard>
  </lifeguard>
  <!-- More.of the same.. -->
</lifeguards>
```

Listing 7.20 lifeguards.xml

You may wish to search for the name of a lifeguard and determine the chain of command up to the highest-level lifeguard. To find the chain of command for any lifeguard shown in Listing 7.20, you would push lifeguards onto the stack as you encountered them, and pop them from the stack when you encountered a `</lifeguard>` tag. When the `<name>` you were looking for was found, you would pop all the elements off the stack and output them to show the chain of command.

Implementing a handler class that uses a stack requires several changes from our previously discussed implementation.

Contents of the Stack

To add a stack to your handler, we first have to create a data structure that our stack will hold. Listing 7.21 illustrates a class, `NodeElements`, designed to maintain information about a given element—mainly, its name, attributes, and character data. You might need more information (e.g., namespace URI and qualified name) or less (e.g., no attributes).

```
class NodeElement {
  private String name;
  private AttributesImpl attlist;
  private StringBuffer buffer;

  public NodeElement(String n, Attributes al) {
    name = n;
    attlist = new AttributesImpl(al);
  }

  public void AddChars(char[] text, int start, int length) {
    buffer.append(text,start,length);
  }

  public String getChars() {
    String chars = (buffer.toString()).trim();
    return chars;
  }

  public String getName() { return name; }

  public Attributes getAL() {
    return (Attributes)attlist;
  }
}
```

Listing 7.21   A node class for storing information about elements

Recall that the `AttributesImpl` helper class is a default implementation of the `Attributes` interface. In this case we are using it to take a persistent snapshot of the element's attributes (passed in the constructor) so that the attributes can be stored in the node.

Maintaining the Stack

A few changes need to be made to the code in the handler class itself. First, import `java.util.Stack` and create a `Stack` instance-level variable:

```
private Stack myStack = new Stack();
```

In `startElement()`, instantiate a node to hold the, element information and push the local name and attributes list onto the stack:

```
public void startElement(String URI, String lName,
    String qName, Attributes attlist) {
  if (lName.equals("name")) {
    myStack.push(new NodeElement(lName, attlist));
  }
}
```

Listing 7.22 startElement() in stack-based SAX handler

In `characters()`, you need to append the characters to the buffer in the node on top of the stack:

```
public void characters(char[] text, int start, int length) {
  if (!myStack.isEmpty()) {
    ((NodeElement)myStack.peek()).AddChars (text,
        start, length);
  }
}
```

Listing 7.23 characters() in stack-based SAX handler

In `endElement()`, you need to pop elements from the stack. It is within `endElement()` that you will generally process information (usually the node you have just popped from the stack) and determine results.

```
public void endElement(String URI, String lName, String qName) {
  NodeElement tempNE = NodeElement(myStack.pop());
  //process tempNE here
}
```

Listing 7.24 endElement() in stack-based SAX handler

For example, with `lifeguards.xml` from Listing 7.20, the code in `endElement()` would check if the name of the lifeguard that was just popped from the stack matched the name you were looking for, and then output the chain of command if it was.

Visual Basic

Visual Basic does not support an intrinsic `Stack` object, but an ordinary `Collection` object will fulfill the purpose. See CN XM000783 for a full Visual Basic version of the above code.

EXAMPLE

The example shown in Listing 7.26 demonstrates a stack-based handler that reads XML documents with a form similar to that shown in Listing 7.25:

```
<employees>
  <employee name="Jane Jones" title="Project Manager">
    <employee name="Fred Smith" title="Technical Lead">
      <employee name="Sally Johnson" title="Developer"/>
      <employee name="Joe Williams" title="Tester"/>
    </employee>
  </employee>
  <!-- More . . .  -->
</employees>
```

Listing 7.25 employees.xml

The handler in Listing 7.26 searches for an employee name and traces the chain of command back to the top-level employee, printing out names and positions of employees.

```
public class stack1 extends DefaultHandler {
  private Stack myStack = new Stack();
  String searchname;

  public void setSearchname(String s) {searchname = s;}

  public void startElement(String URI, String lName,
      String qName, Attributes attlist) {
    myStack.push(new NodeElement(lName, attlist));
  }

  public void endElement(String URI, String lName,
      String qName) {
```

```
      NodeElement top = (NodeElement)myStack.peek();
      Attributes al = top.getAL();
      String nameTop = al.getValue("", "name");
      if (lName.equals("employee") &&
          nameTop.equals(searchname)) {
        for (int i = myStack.size() - 1; i >= 0 &&
            ((NodeElement) myStack.get(i)).getName().equals (
            "employee"); i--) {
          NodeElement localNode = (NodeElement)myStack.get(i);
          Attributes localAL = localNode.getAL();
          String localName = localAL.getValue("", "name");
          String localPos = localAL.getValue("", "title");
          System.out.println(localName + " (" + localPos + ")");
        }
      }
      myStack.pop();
  }
}
```

Listing 7.26 stack1.java

If we implemented this handler and used it to search for the employee name "Joe Williams," the output would look like this:

```
Joe Williams (Tester)
Fred Smith (Technical Lead)
Jane Jones (Project Manager)
```

Listing 7.27 output from stack1.java

The code to perform the same task on an XML document in which `<employee>` elements contain children with name and position data as characters (instead of attributes) is slightly different, and longer. It can be found at CodeNotes Pointer CN XM000703.

SUMMARY

Stack-based event handlers allow you to maintain ancestor information that you would not normally be able to maintain in SAX. Stacks are extremely useful for parsing recursive XML documents where different levels of similar nodes exist.

Topic: Features

SAX2 adds mechanisms called *features,* which allow your application to request arbitrary functionality from the parser. Features allow you to configure how the SAX parser behaves during parsing. The two most commonly requested features are validation and namespace support. Activating validation allows the parser to validate an XML document against its DTD or schema (Chapter 8) as it parses. Namespace support provides the `startElement()` and `endElement()` methods with additional information concerning the namespace in which an element exists. We will discuss namespaces later in this chapter.

Note that MSXML 3.0 does *not* support the DTD/schema validation feature.

CONCEPTS

Requesting Features

The `XMLReader` interface has two methods for requesting and determining that a particular feature is turned on or off: `getFeature()` and `setFeature()`. The standard format for getting or setting a SAX feature is:

```
parser.getFeature("feature URL");
parser.setFeature("feature URL", [true/false]);
```

The `getFeature()` method returns a boolean indicating whether the feature is currently enabled. The `setFeature()` method can be used to toggle the setting and enable or disable a particular feature. If you try to use `setFeature()` or `getFeature()` on an unrecognized or unsupported feature, an exception (`SAXNotRecognizedException`) will be thrown. The VB `XMLReader` object supports `putFeature()` instead of `setFeature()`, although the parameters are the same.

Core Features

Creators of SAX parsers can add any new features they wish to their XMLReaders. However, there is a core set of features that every SAX parser should support. The two most often used features:

- http://xml.org/sax/features/namespaces, which controls general namespace processing in the parser. (See the Namespaces topic later in this chapter.)
- http://xml.org/sax/features/validation, which indicates whether or not the parser should validate the document against a DTD or

schema. If validation is on, documents that do not conform to their DTDs will throw exceptions.

Other core features exist but are not as commonly used. Details and examples for some of these features can be found on the CodeNotes website XM000704.

EXAMPLE

The following example will query the parser as to whether it is currently validating or not:

```
public boolean isValidating (XMLReader parser) {
  if (parser.getFeature
      ("http://xml.org.sax.features.validation")) {
    return true;
  } else {return false;}
}
```

Listing 7.28 Querying a parser's validation feature

SUMMARY

Features add configurable extensions to `XMLReader` instances. Features can be set using the XMLReader's `setFeature()` method, and can be checked using the XMLReader's `getFeature()` method. The two most valuable features are validation support (which toggles whether the parser will compare a document to its DTD as it parses) and namespace support (which toggles whether or not a parser will pass namespace information to the handler methods).

Topic: Error Handling

This chapter has not included error-handling code in its examples in the interest of brevity. However, you will want your own programs to behave intelligently on failure, so it is now time to turn our attention to error handling. This section covers the SAX `ErrorHandler` interface and SAX exception classes.

Note that most of this topic does not apply to Visual Basic. Visual

Basic does not, as of version 6, have support for exceptions. See this topic's Bugs and Caveats section for more details.

CONCEPTS

Exceptions

When a SAX method fails, it will generally throw a `SAXException` or one of its subclasses. The three exception subclasses are:

- ***SAXNotSupportedException***, which is thrown when you try to set or query a SAX feature that exists but is not supported by your particular parser.
- ***SAXNotRecognizedException***, which is thrown when you try to set or query a SAX feature that does not exist.
- ***SAXParseException***, which is thrown when the parser encounters XML that is not well-formed. By implementing the `ErrorHandler` interface, you decide what happens when `SAXParseExceptions` are thrown. See the ErrorHandler Interface, below, for how to implement this interface.

By default, SAX handles errors by throwing `SAXExceptions`. All of your SAX handler methods should throw `SAXExceptions`. If a `SAXException` occurs during parsing, the parse process will halt unless you specify otherwise explicitly.

The ErrorHandler Interface

SAX parsing errors can be handled explicitly by registering an error handler object that implements `ErrorHandler`. You can use your `DefaultHandler` object (which implements `ErrorHandler`'s methods), or create an entirely new class just for handling errors. `ErrorHandler` is useful if you want to locate where parsing errors occur within an XML document.

To register an error handler, use the `XMLReader's setErrorHandler()` method.

```
parser.setErrorHandler(errorhandler);
```

If you do not register an error handler, XML parsing errors will not be reported. When a critical error occurs (ending the parse), the SAX parser will simply stop processing the document.

The `ErrorHandler` interface contains only three callback methods.

error()

Errors occur when a document cannot be validated against its declared grammar. For example, if an `XMLReader` is validating, it will report an error if the document being parsed does not conform to its DTD or schema. By default, the `XMLReader` should continue parsing if an error is detected. If you explicitly throw an exception within the `error()` method, the `XMLReader` will stop parsing. The `error()` method is generally used to report the type and location of a discrepancy within the XML document's grammar, without ending the parse.

This code shows the prototype for `error()`:

```
public void error(SAXParseException e) throws SAXException {}
```

fatalError()

Fatal errors occur when an XML document being parsed is not well-formed. Fatal errors should almost always cause the parser to stop reporting events. By default, all parsers will cease after a fatal error is detected (regardless of whether you explicitly throw an exception or not), assuming that the document is unusable.

This code shows the prototype for `fatalError()`:

```
public void fatalError(SAXParseException e)
        throws SAXException {}
```

warning()

Warnings are the result of minor problems, such as XML that does not conform to the more strict SGML standards from which XML is derived. Warnings do not (and should not) stop parsing. The `warning()` method rarely needs to be implemented. XML parsers are inconsistent about what causes them to issue warnings.

This code shows the prototype for `warning()`:

```
public void warning(SAXParseException e) throws SAXException {}
```

SAXParseException

`SAXParseException` contains useful methods for determining the location of an error or fatal error in an XML document.

- `getColumnNumber()` returns the column in which the exception occurred.
- `getLineNumber()` returns the line in which the exception occurred.
- `getPublicId()` returns the public identifier of the document.
- `getSystemId()` returns the system identifier of the document.

EXAMPLE

Enabling Validation

Listing 7.29 shows how to enable validation in your parser, if it is supported, and uses the `SAXNotSupported` and `SAXNotRecognized` exceptions to report errors.

```
try {
  parser.setFeature (
      "http://xml.org/sax/features/validation",true);
}
/** if you try and set this feature and the parser is
not a validating parser, an exception is thrown **/
catch (SAXNotSupportedException e) {
  System.out.println("Parser does not support validation.");
}
/** if the parser does not recognize the validation
feature (this should not happen) … **/
catch (SAXNotRecognizedException e) {
  System.out.println("Feature not recognized.");
}
```

Listing 7.29 Enabling validation and handling related exceptions

This code fragment would be used in the function that creates the parser instance (e.g., the `main()` function in Listing 7.2).

Reporting Validity Errors

The next example shows how to use an `ErrorHandler` method to report the location of a validation error in an XML document. This code fragment would be used in an `ErrorHandler` implementation that you have attached to an `XMLReader` instance, using `setErrorHandler()`:

```
public void error(SAXParseException e) throws SAXException {
  System.err.println("XML does not conform to DTD in " +
      e.getSystemId() + " on line " + e.getLineNumber() +
      ", column " + e.getColumnNumber());
  throw e;
}
```

Listing 7.30 Reporting the location of a validity error

Note that we explicitly throw an exception in this method (`throw e;`), meaning that the parser will stop parsing when it encounters a validity error. If we didn't throw an exception, `error()` would output the location of the error, and the parse would continue.

BUGS AND CAVEATS

SAX Errors in MSXML3

MSXML3 supports only `fatalError()`:

```
Sub fatalError(oLocator As IVBSAXLocator, _
    strError As String, nErrorCode As Long)
```

The column and line numbers are available through the `oLocator` object as opposed to the `SAXParseException` class.

Handling Fatal Errors

One drawback to SAX has to do with complications that result from the handling of fatal errors partway through processing. There are several ways to handle this situation gracefully:

1. Parse the document twice, once to make sure that the document is well formed (and possibly valid), and again to perform the actual processing.
2. You may be able to take advantage of transactional capabilities. When writing to an SQL database, for example, you might begin a transaction on `startDocument()`, commit on `endDocument()`, and rollback on `fatalError()`. Long-running transactions can bog down your database, however. Use this option only when the entire processing operation is quite short.
3. Design your handler to keep a record of what methods have been called, and do your processing later. For example, if you were reading from an XML document and inserting into a database, you could implement your handler methods such that they record the SQL statements in a `LinkedList` as the document parsed, rather than executing them on the fly. Upon receiving `endDocument()`, you would then run down the list and execute all the SQL statements at once.

SUMMARY

Exceptions in SAX are handled by `SAXException` and its three subclasses, which are `SAXNotRecognizedException`, `SAXNotSupportedException`, and `SAXParseException`. Parse exceptions can be handled by the `ErrorHandler` interface, whose methods you can implement to perform actions you deem appropriate. These customized error methods are useful for locating the source of an error in an XML document.

Topic: Namespaces

SAX2 supports namespaces for elements and attributes. Namespace information is available within the `startElement()` and `endElement()` methods as two strings: a namespace URL and a qualified name. Namespace information can be used to make the SAX parser distinguish between elements and attributes in different namespaces, and process them separately. Namespace support is also useful when processing higher-level XML documents, such as XSL stylesheets or XML schemas with SAX.

Namespaces are discussed in full in the Namespaces topic of Chapter 3. If you don't know what namespaces are and how they are used in XML, you should read that topic before continuing with this one.

CONCEPTS

Activating Namespace Support

By default, SAX XMLReaders support namespaces. You can turn off namespace support with the following line of code:

```
parser.setFeature("http://xml.org/features/namespaces", false);
```

When namespace support is on (true), namespace URLs and local names will be reported to `startElement()` and `endElement()`. When namespace support is off (false), attempting to access namespace URLs and local names within these methods may result in null values or errors.

Activating Namespace Prefix Support

Recall that qualified names are element or attribute names attached to a prefix. For example, `doc:book` is an example of a qualified name where doc is the namespace, and book is an attribute associated with the doc namespace. Qualified names are useful for processing XML documents such as XSL stylesheets and XML schemas. By default, SAX XMLReaders do not pass in qualified names of elements and attributes when they call handler methods. This means that attempting to access the qualified name in `startElement()` or `endElement()` may result in null values or errors. You can toggle on namespace prefix support with the following line of code:

```
parser.setFeature(
    "http://xml.org/features/namespace-prefixes", true);
```

SUMMARY

Table 7.1 shows what `startElement()` and `endElement()` will receive as arguments depending on whether namespaces and namespace prefixes are activated. Namespace support is on by default, and namespace prefix support is off by default (shown in bold).

name-spaces	name-space prefixes	URL	Local Name	Qname
On	On	http://www.website.com/ns/	name	pre:name
On	**Off**	**http://www.website.com/ns/**	**name**	**empty string**
Off	On	empty string	empty string	pre:name
Off	Off	ILLEGAL CONFIGURATION		

Table 7.1 Namespace and namespace prefix support in SAX2

The attributes of each element will contain similar information.

Namespace support is a new feature of SAX2, and allows more specific handling of elements and attributes by allowing the parser to distinguish between elements and attributes in different namespaces.

Chapter Summary

The Simple API for XML (SAX) provides a fast, lightweight approach to XML processing. SAX processes XML documents by reading them one piece at a time and making callbacks into your application. The pieces, which are things like element start- and end-tags or character data, are then processed by methods in a handler class. You create a handler class and define the methods within it to process the data as you see fit.

SAX2, the focus of this chapter, adds support for namespaces, filtering, and features in its parsing and handling interfaces. Namespaces can now be given, fully qualified, to your handler methods; pluggable filters allow you to modularize your handling of XML documents CN XM000790; and features allow you to customize how your parser behaves. SAX is an excellent choice for rapid, stateless processing of large XML documents for which you don't require random access. You can find links to the SAX specification on the CodeNotes website CN XM000706.

Chapter 8

XML SCHEMAS

XML schemas are templates for XML documents; they allow you to specify valid arrangement of the elements and attributes within an XML document, and to impose limits on their contents. Schemas help to ensure structural consistency across groups of XML documents.

If you have read about Document Type Definitions (DTDs) in Chapter 3, you should already understand the need for XML document templates. Templates ensure that XML documents conform to a set standard. You can reference one template from many XML documents in order to guarantee uniformity. Both DTDs and XML schemas provide this functionality by allowing you to define the structure of an XML document exactly, thereby restricting document creators from expanding an XML document beyond its intended purpose.

XML schemas, however, go several steps beyond DTDs. Schemas allow the creation of new data types, more specific limitation of element and attribute contents, inheritance of one data type by another, and more.

The XML schema recommendation was created by the W3C to replace DTDs, which lack flexibility and expressiveness and, unlike schemas, are not proper XML grammars. The XML Schema Primer Recommendation may be found at http://www.w3.org/TR/xmlschema-0.

If you have not read the Namespaces and Document Type Definitions topics in Chapter 3, it is recommended that you do so before reading this chapter. Namespaces, in particular, play an extremely important role in XML schemas.

SIMPLE APPLICATION

Because DTDs and XML schemas perform the same basic function, it is often helpful to see a comparison of the two.

The two examples in this section (Listings 8.2 and 8.3) both provide a template for the XML in Listing 8.1 (`person.xml`). Note that `person.xml` contains references to both a DTD and an XML schema. Typically, you'd use only one or the other, but both are technically allowed in one document. We'll discuss linking documents to an XML schema in the first topic of this chapter.

```
<?xml version="1.0"?>
<!-- DTD reference -->
<!DOCTYPE person SYSTEM "person.dtd">
<!-- Schema reference -->
<person xmlns="http://www.person.com"
    xmlns:xsi="http://www.w3.org/2001/XMLSchema-instance"
    xsi:schemaLocation="http://www.person.com person.xsd">
  <firstname>Craig</firstname>
  <lastname>Wills</lastname>
  <birthday>1978-01-12</birthday>
  <weight>-175</weight>
</person>
```

Listing 8.1 person.xml

If you think you noticed a mistake in `person.xml` (the negative weight), you're correct; we'll explain why it's there in a moment.

First, let's look the DTD and XML schema that provide the template for `person.xml`. The DTD in Listing 8.2 provides a template for the elements in `person.xml`. Note that the attribute list for `<person>` declared in `person.dtd` must exist to account for the schema reference in `person.xml`'s root element. This attribute list is only required because we reference both a DTD and a schema in the same document.

```
<!ELEMENT person (firstname,lastname,birthday,weight)>
<!ELEMENT firstname (#PCDATA)>
<!ELEMENT lastname (#PCDATA)>
<!ELEMENT birthday (#PCDATA)>
<!ELEMENT weight (#PCDATA)>
<!ATTLIST person xmlns CDATA #REQUIRED
                 xmlns:xsi CDATA #REQUIRED
                 xsi:schemaLocation CDATA #REQUIRED>
```

Listing 8.2 person.dtd

Listing 8.3 (`person.xsd`) is an XML schema that provides almost the same template as the DTD in Listing 8.2. The sole difference is that `person.xsd` declares *data types* for each element in `person.xml`—it says that the `<firstname>` and `<lastname>` elements must contain strings (`xsd:string`); that the `<birthday>` element must contain a date (we'll see later in this chapter that dates must be in the form CCYY-MM-DD); and that the `<weight>` element must contain an unsigned integer (i.e., it must be 0, or positive).

```
<?xml version="1.0"?>

<xsd:schema xmlns:xsd="http://www.w3.org/2001/XMLSchema"
    targetNamespace="http://www.person.com"
    xmlns="http://www.person.com"
    elementFormDefault="qualified">
  <xsd:element name="person">
    <xsd:complexType>
      <xsd:sequence>
        <xsd:element name="firstname" type="xsd:string"/>
        <xsd:element name="lastname" type="xsd:string"/>
        <xsd:element name="birthday" type="xsd:date"/>
        <xsd:element name="weight" type="xsd:unsignedInt"/>
      </xsd:sequence>
    </xsd:complexType>
  </xsd:element>
</xsd:schema>
```

Listing 8.3 person.xsd

If we validate `person.xml` against its DTD (for example, by parsing it using a validating DOM or SAX parser), it will validate perfectly, as all the elements and attributes within it conform to the DTD.

However, if we try to validate it against the XML schema, the `person.xml` document will be invalid, because the weight value is the wrong datatype.

If you want to use an XML editor like XML Spy, discussed in Chapter 3 (XML Essentials), you can simply load `person.xml` into the editor and use the editor's validation function to see if the document is considered valid. We'll use XSV (the command-line validator, discussed in Chapter 2) to show what happens when we try to validate `person.xml` against `person.xsd`.

From a command line, go to the directory in which XSV is installed (or make certain XSV is in your PATH) and type `"xsv person.xml"`. (You'll need to use the correct path to `person.xml` if it is not in the same directory). XSV should output its processing information as an XML document, shown in Listing 8.4:

```
C:\xsv>xsv person.xml
<?xml version='1.0'?>
<xsv docElt='{http://www.person.com}person'
instanceAssessed='true' instanceErrors='1'
rootType='[Anonymous]' schemaErrors='0'
schemaLocs='http://www.person.com -> person.xsd'
target='file:/C:/xsv/person.xml' validation='strict'
version='XSV 1.195/1.97 of 2001/06/09 19:14:08'
xmlns='http://www.w3.org/2000/05/xsv'>
<importAttempt URI='file:/C:/xsv/person.xsd'
namespace='http://www.person.com' outcome='success'/>
<invalid char='3' code='cvc-complex-type.1.2.2' line='11'
resource='file:/C:/xsv/person.xml'>element content failed type
check: -175&#60;0</invalid>
</xsv>
```

Listing 8.4 Output of XSV processing of person.xml

The last element in the XML shown in Listing 8.4 is an `<invalid>` element (shown in bold), which indicates that XSV has found an error in the XML document. In this case, it has found that an element has an invalid value: the `<weight>` element has a value below 0 (it's –175, as opposed to 175), which is illegal for an unsigned integer.

Whereas the DTD did not catch this mistake, the XML schema enforces much stronger data typing, and can therefore be used to control more strictly the content of your XML documents. Change the value of the `<weight>` element in `person.xml` to 175, and revalidate to ensure that the XML document now conforms to its schema.

CORE CONCEPTS

Schemas are XML

All XML schemas are, themselves, legal XML documents. Like XSLT and XHTML, XML schemas are *grammars* of XML. This means that XML schemas can be read, parsed, or edited by any application that can read, parse, or edit XML.

One of the main reasons that the W3C created the XML schema recommendation is that DTD syntax is inconsistent with XML syntax, so parsers and editors must contain additional functionality specifically for handling DTDs. XML schema, along with other W3C-planned recommendations such as XSL-FO (an XML-based replacement for CSS), are steps toward the W3C's goal of having all XML-related technologies follow the same grammar.

Improvements over DTDs

XML schemas are a marked improvement over DTDs. Some of the more prominent improvements include:

- Data Types—Whereas DTD data types are of little use for validating the contents of attributes (and of no use at all for validating the text data of elements), XML schemas provide several dozen useful built-in data types, including integers, dates, and URLs. This is, perhaps, the single most compelling feature that XML schemas offer over DTDs.
- Custom Data Types—Schemas support the ability to create your own data types, either from scratch or by inheriting from existing data types. For example, you could create a `celcius` data type that would inherit the properties of a `float`, but be restricted in that it could not contain a value below –273 (absolute zero).
- Element Grouping—Schemas provide the ability to express sets of elements, unique elements, substitutable elements, unions between elements, and more.

Schema Validators

XML schemas, like DTDs, require that an application use a *validating parser* in order to identify inconsistencies between an XML document and its referenced schema. Major browsers such as Internet Explorer and Netscape do not yet contain validating parsers at the time of this writing. However, many XML editors now support XML schemas and will allow you to validate your documents. The Viewing and Editing XML Documents section in Chapter 3 details several good XML editors, most of which have XML schema-validation capabilities. Additionally, two other tools with schema support (available as of this writing) are:

- **Apache XML Project's Xerces XML parser**, which can be used with DOM (Chapter 6) or SAX (Chapter 7) to validate XML documents against schemas while parsing and processing them.
- **Language Technology Group's XSV 1.2**, an XML schema validator available as a self-installing WIN32 application, or as a web-based form.

Links to download both of these tools can be found on the CodeNotes website, at CN XM00802. See also the W3C's links to schema tools at http://www.w3.org/XML/Schema.

Topic: Basic Schema Design

All XML schemas and the XML documents that reference them must contain certain key elements in order to work together. An XML document must contain information to reference its schema, and an XML schema must contain namespace declarations in order for its contents to be recognized as XML schema grammar. Both documents and schemas need to reference particular namespaces if they are to be validated by a schema-enabled parser. This topic will cover the basic design of an XML schema and its referencing XML document.

CONCEPTS

Declaring a Schema

You can think of a schema as a vocabulary contained within a namespace. Each schema you create must declare a namespace into which its element and attribute declarations must fall. For example, you could specify that all the elements and attributes you declare in your schema should fall under the `http://www.mysite.com` namespace. This namespace would then contain the vocabulary that you could use within documents that reference this schema.

Additionally, the schema requires a vocabulary that you use to define your elements and attributes. For example, the `<complexType>` element is an element in the XML schema vocabulary, used to declare a particular type of element. In order for a schema to be able to use this "metavocabulary," it must associate these special schema-specific elements with a namespace.

The following is an example of a typical schema declaration:

```
<xsd:schema xmlns:xsd="http://www.w3.org/2001/XMLSchema"
            targetNamespace="http://www.mysite.com"
            xmlns="http://www.mysite.com"
            elementFormDefault="qualified">
```

Listing 8.5 A typical schema declaration

This element declaration can be broken down into five parts, which we will now discuss.

XML Schema Root Element

The root element of an XML schema must always be `<schema>`. This indicates to the parser that the schema declaration is beginning. Because `<schema>` is an element within the XML schema vocabulary, it is qualified with the prefix you associate with the XMLSchema namespace: `<xsd:schema>`. The `xsd` prefix is described in the next section.

XMLSchema Namespace

The XMLSchema namespace is `http://www.w3.org/2001/XMLSchema`. This namespace contains the vocabulary used within a schema to define elements and attributes. This namespace is sometimes said to represent a "schema for schemas," and should be recognized by all schema-validating parsers. Parsers recognizing this namespace would know to validate the schema itself against the "schema for schemas," in order to ensure that the grammar used conforms to the XML schema specification.

In our example in Listing 8.5, the `XMLSchema` namespace is associated with the prefix `xsd`. All elements and attributes in this schema that are prefixed with `xsd` will be recognized by the parser as XML schema vocabulary, and will be validated to ensure that they conform to the XML schema specification.

```
<xsd:schema xmlns:xsd="http://www.w3.org/2001/XMLSchema">
```

The "xsd" prefix is not mandated by the standard; you can choose any prefix you like. However, using "xsd" is common practice.

Target Namespace

As we will see later in the chapter, it is possible to define complex data types (data types containing other data types), format restrictions, and other declarations in a schema that an XML document will want to reference. Because an XML document may make use of more than one schema, it is best to place these schema entities into a namespace of their own, one that the XML document can reference unambiguously. Specifically, the namespace that contains entities in a schema is referred to as a *target namespace*. The target namespace can be thought of as a container for schema declarations. An XML document that wants to reach in to this container can use the element and attribute declarations in the target namespace as its *vocabulary*. This namespace can be any unique URI that you want to use to identify your new vocabulary.

In Listing 8.5, the target namespace for the vocabulary defined by the schema is `http://www.mysite.com`.

```
<xsd:schema targetNamespace="http://www.mysite.com">
```

Note that unqualified elements and attributes in the schema are not automatically placed within the target namespace. The reserved `targetNamespace` attribute simply dictates where the vocabulary you are defining will exist. In order to force elements and attributes to go into this namespace, you need to declare what is known as a *default namespace*.

The target namespace is the namespace that the XML document will reference, whereas the default namespace is the namespace container inside the XML schema. In other words, when an XML document references the schema, it will use the target namespace to unambiguously resolve and refer to schema elements. However, within the schema, unqualified elements will fall into the default namespace.

Default Namespace

Schemas should provide a default namespace for the elements and attributes they define. Once a default namespace is defined, all unqualified elements and attributes (within the schema) will automatically be placed in the default namespace.

Usually, the default namespace will be the same as the target namespace, so that unqualified elements and attributes will automatically fall into the target namespace and become part of the vocabulary being defined.

A typical default namespace declaration looks like this:

```
<xsd:schema xmlns="http://www.mysite.com">
```

If you do not declare a default namespace, your elements and attributes will not be considered to be in a namespace and will not become part of the new vocabulary. Having elements and attributes that are not in a namespace can cause problems. See the Bugs and Caveats section of this topic for more details.

elementFormDefault

The `elementFormDefault` attribute specifies whether or not XML documents that reference this schema must qualify their elements (with the namespace identifier). The default value for this attribute is "unqualified", meaning that global elements (those elements declared directly under the <xsd:schema> root element) must be qualified in the XML document, but that local elements (elements declared within global elements) must not be qualified in the XML document.

By setting elementFormDefault="qualified", you can force qualification of all elements in an XML document referencing your schema. You can then avoid having to explicitly qualify some elements and not others by defining a default namespace in your XML. Forcing qualification has the advantage of making your XML schema more flexible by allowing you to change global elements into local elements without affecting all the XML documents referencing your schema. We will discuss global and local elements again later in this chapter.

The attributeFormDefault attribute (not shown in Listing 8.5) works in a similar manner. Its default value is "unqualified", but if you set it to "qualified", XML documents referencing the schema will be forced to qualify all attributes that appear in the schema.

Referencing a Schema

An XML document that references a schema is called an *instance* of that schema. An instance of a schema can use only the vocabulary defined by that schema. If it strays from what the schema defines, it will no longer be valid, and a validating parser will indicate an error.

Typically, the reference to a schema is placed in the root element. A reference to a schema within an XML document will look something like this:

```
<root xmlns="http://www.mysite.com"
    xmlns:xsi="http://www.w3.org/2001/XMLSchema-instance"
    xsi:schemaLocation="http://www.mysite.org mysite.xsd">
```

Listing 8.6 An XML document referencing a schema

This reference can be broken up into three parts, which are the following:

Default Namespace Declaration

The default namespace declaration tells a schema instance that all elements and attributes within this XML document, by default, will exist in the default namespace. For example, this XML declares that all unqualified elements and attributes in this instance exist in the http://www.mysite.com namespace.

```
<root xmlns="http://www.mysite.com">
```

This namespace should be the target namespace that was declared in the schema you will be using. The default namespace declaration tells the schema instance where its vocabulary will come from.

Note that if, in your schema, you had set `elementFormDefault="unqualified"`, you would have to associate a prefix with this namespace instead of defining a default namespace. You would then have to qualify the root element with that prefix. This alternate arrangement would look like the following:

```
<sch:root xmlns:sch="http://www.mysite.com">
```

All root level elements would then have to be qualified with the `"sch"` prefix.

Schema Instance Declaration

As previously stated, XML documents referencing a schema are called instances of that schema. Every schema instance must provide a location of the schema it is using. However, the attribute used to provide this location is a member of a special `XMLSchema-instance` namespace. So, before you can point to where the schema is, you must first declare a prefix to be associated with the `XMLSchema-instance` namespace. This declaration should look something like this:

```
<root xmlns:xsi="http://www.w3.org/2001/XMLSchema-instance">
```

This declaration associates the prefix `xsi` with the `XMLSchema-instance` namespace. You can now use attributes within this namespace, as you will see next.

Schema Location

Once you have a prefix associated with the `XMLSchema-instance` namespace, you can use the `schemaLocation` attribute, which exists in the vocabulary defined by `XMLSchema-instance`. This attribute defines the location of the XML schema that the document uses to restrict its attributes and elements. The `schemaLocation` attribute is used as follows:

```
<root xmlns:xsi=http://www.w3.org/2001/XMLSchema-instance
    xsi:schemaLocation="http://www.mysite.com mysite.xsd">
```

The declaration states that this document should follow the rules defined in `mysite.xsd`. Note that the `<xsi:schemaLocation>` attribute actually contains two values, separated by a space: first, the target namespace of the schema, and second, the actual location of the schema.

Multiple Validations

You may have noticed by now that XML schemas use multiple levels of validation. First, a validating parser will validate the schema itself against the vocabulary defined in the XMLSchema namespace (which any application using this parser should recognize). Second, the parser validates instances of the schema against the vocabulary in the schema's target namespace.

This "multiple validation" ensures not only that your documents are valid but that your schemas are valid, as well. Thus, applications implementing your schemas will not encounter difficulties with vocabulary that cannot be interpreted.

EXAMPLE

The following example illustrates a very basic schema and XML document that uses the schema. First, we'll look again at a simple XML schema that includes a full set of namespace declarations.

```
<?xml version="1.0"?>

<xsd:schema xmlns:xsd="http://www.w3.org/2001/XMLSchema"
    targetNamespace="http://www.person.org"
    xmlns="http://www.person.org">
  <xsd:element name="person" type="xsd:string"/>
</xsd:schema>
```

Listing 8.7 person.xsd

Element and attribute declarations will be discussed in the next topic. For now, however, all you need to know is that this schema declares that its instances can contain only one element, `<person>`, which in turn can contain only character data. This single rule is the schema's vocabulary, which is represented by the namespace `http://www.person.org`.

The following is a valid XML document, according to the schema declared in Listing 8.7.

```
<?xml version="1.0"?>

<person xmlns="http://www.person.org"
    xmlns:xsi="http://www.w3.org/2001/XMLSchema-instance"
```

```
    xsi:schemaLocation="http://www.person.org person.xsd">
  Arthur Philip Dent
</person>
```

Listing 8.8 person.xml, referencing person.xsd

This XML document is an instance of `person.xsd`, and derives its vocabulary from the namespace `http://www.person.org`, declared in `person.xsd`.

BUGS AND CAVEATS

Always Specify a targetNamespace

The `targetNamespace` attribute is actually an optional attribute in the `<xsd:schema>` element. An XML schema without a target namespace is sometimes referred to as being in a "chameleon" namespace. You will read about combining XML schemas later in this chapter, in the Practical XML Schema Features topic. If you try to combine an XML schema that is not in a namespace with another schema, it will be difficult, if not impossible, to reference the declarations made in the chameleon namespace, because you will not be able to associate it with a prefix (i.e., there is nothing with which to associate the prefix!). In other words, these hidden elements may disappear and become inaccessible.

HOW AND WHY

Why Won't My Schema Validate?

Older XML schema validators may use an older version of the XML schema recommendation, with a different namespace. If you have problems validating with `http://www.w3.org/2001/XMLSchema`, try using `http://www.w3.org/2000/10/XMLSchema` instead.

SUMMARY

XML schemas and their instances follow a certain format for declaration and referencing. Namespaces play a crucial role in XML schemas and are used to represent vocabularies defined within XML schemas. Schema instances must reference the schemas themselves, as well as the target (vocabulary) namespaces defined within them, in order to determine what elements and attributes they are allowed to use.

Topic: Elements and Attributes

XML schemas define what attributes and elements an XML document can have, in what order they must occur, and what their contents can be. Element and attribute declarations in schemas tend to be much longer than their DTD equivalents. The added volume is made up for, however, by the increased extensibility offered by XML schemas. For instance, schemas allow you to declare what the character content of an element must look like whereas DTDs can declare only that an element contains character content.

This topic will cover basic XML schema element and attribute declarations. The more complex nuances of element and attribute data typing will be covered in the next topic, Data Types.

CONCEPTS

Elements

XML schemas allow much more flexibility concerning the manner in which elements can be declared than do DTDs. To begin with, the XML schema grammar allows two basic types of elements: elements with simple content, and elements with complex content. Both types are discussed next.

Simple Elements

Simple content elements are defined as elements that can contain only text, and may not contain other elements. The format of the text within simple elements can be defined in many different ways, but these elements can never contain children. An example of a simple element declaration follows:

```
<xsd:element name="person" type="xsd:string"/>
```

In the example above, the empty `<xsd:element>` tag indicates that the declaration of a simple element will follow. The `name` attribute declares the name of the element (person). The `type` attribute declares the data type of this element (string). (Data types will be covered in the next topic.) For now, notice that both `element` and `string` are qualified with the `xsd` prefix; both of these are terms in the XML schema vocabulary. A DTD declaration for the same element would look like this:

```
<!ELEMENT person (#PCDATA)>
```

Note that in the DTD definition, the data type is simply Parsed Character Data (PCDATA), which can contain anything.

Complex Elements

Complex content elements can contain other elements. The following is an example of a complex element declaration:

```
<xsd:element name="person">
  <xsd:complexType>
    <xsd:sequence>
      <xsd:element name="name" type="xsd:string"/>
      <xsd:element name="id" type="xsd:integer"/>
      <xsd:element name="birthday" type="xsd:date"/>
    </xsd:sequence>
  </xsd:complexType>
</xsd:element>
```

Listing 8.9 Complex element declaration

The schema fragment in Listing 8.9 declares a complex element, `<person>`, which contains three simple elements, `<name>`, `<id>`, and `<birthday>`. The `<xsd:sequence>` element indicates that the three simple elements must occur in that specific order (we'll discuss sequences later in this topic). The following DTD declaration is similar to the schema declaration in Listing 8.9, although the data typing is not nearly as strong:

```
<!ELEMENT person (name,id,birthday)>
<!ELEMENT name (#PCDATA)>
<!ELEMENT id (#PCDATA)>
<!ELEMENT birthday (#PCDATA)>
```

Occurrence Restraints

It is often desirable to restrict the number of child elements allowed within a parent. For example, you might want to declare that a `<house>` element can contain up to ten `<resident>` elements, and no more. DTDs allow you only to specify that an element can occur zero, one, or unlimited times (although you can "trick" them into allowing elements to occur *n* times by manually typing out *n-1* entries—e.g., `dog,dog?,dog?)` for one to three `dog` elements). Schemas, on the other hand, are much easier to use—simply supply the `minOccurs` and `maxOccurs` attributes of `<xsd:element>`. These attributes are called *occurrence restraints.*

For example, we can implement the `<house>` and `<residence>` restrictions from the last paragraph with the following complex element declaration:

```
<xsd:element name="house">
  <xsd:complexType>
    <xsd:sequence>
      <xsd:element name="resident" type="xsd:string"
          minOccurs="1" maxOccurs="10"/>
    </xsd:sequence>
  </xsd:complexType>
</xsd:element>
```

Listing 8.10 Demonstration of occurrence restraints

You can include one, both, or neither of these occurrence restraint attributes when declaring an element. The default value for both `minOccurs` and `maxOccurs` is 1. Therefore, if you do not specify values in your schema, the child element will be unique and mandatory within its parent. Note that if you want to allow unlimited instances of an element, you can use `maxOccurs="unbounded"`. On the other hand, if you want the element to be optional, set `minOccurs="0"`.

Sequence and All

In the previous examples of complex elements (Listings 8.9 and 8.10), the children of the elements being defined were always contained within `<xsd:sequence>` elements. Placing elements within a sequence implies that instances of the schema must implement these elements in exactly the order in which they appear within the schema. For example, the following schema fragment says that the elements of a shipping order, `<from>`, `<to>`, and `<sent>` must occur in that order:

```
<xsd:sequence>
  <xsd:element name="from" type="xsd:string"/>
  <xsd:element name="to" type="xsd:string"/>
  <xsd:element name="sent" type="xsd:date"/>
</xsd:sequence>
```

Listing 8.11 A strict sequence with the xsd:sequence element

You can allow XML document creators to choose the order in which they include elements by using the `<xsd:all>` element. `<xsd:all>` implies that any elements defined within the `<xsd:all>` tag can occur in any order. The following schema fragment says that `<name>`, `<rank>`, and `<serial_number>` elements can occur in any order within the parent element:

```
<xsd:all>
  <xsd:element name="name" type="xsd:string"/>
  <xsd:element name="rank" type="xsd:string"/>
  <xsd:element name="serial_number" type="xsd:integer"/>
</xsd:all>
```

Listing 8.12 Arbitrary order with the xsd:all element

Note that `<xsd:all>` does not allow you to specify a `maxOccurs` greater than 1. In other words, when `<xsd:all>` is used, `maxOccurs` must always be set to 1, and `minOccurs` may be 0 or 1, indicating that the element is optional.

Choice

If you want to allow XML document creators the choice between two or more elements, you can use the `<xsd:choice>` schema element. For example, the following schema fragment allows either a `<state>` or a `<province>` element to appear within the parent element, but not both:

```
<xsd:choice>
  <xsd:element name="state" type="xsd:string"/>
  <xsd:element name="province" type="xsd:string"/>
</xsd:choice>
```

Listing 8.13 Using the xsd:choice tag

The fragment in listing 8.13 is similar to this DTD declaration:

```
<!ELEMENT [elementname] (state | province)>
```

The `<xsd:sequence>` and `<xsd:choice>` elements also allow you to specify how many occurrences of each subelement can occur, using `maxOccurs` and `minOccurs` attributes as described in the previous section.

Attributes

XML schemas allow you to declare attributes for use within instances. Schema attribute declarations are made in much the same way as element declarations. One major difference between element and attribute declarations is that attributes can have only simple content. Obviously, attributes cannot contain other attributes (or elements).

A typical attribute declaration in an XML schema could look like this:

```
<xsd:attribute name="empid" type="xsd:integer" use="required"/>
```

Listing 8.14 A simple attribute declaration

We'll break down this declaration into parts:

Name
First, the `<xsd:attribute>` element is used to signify that an attribute is being declared. The `name` attribute of this element is, obviously, the name of the attribute being declared.

Type
The `type` attribute indicates the data type of the attribute being declared. Data types will be discussed in greater detail in the next topic.

Use
The `use` element indicates whether or not the attribute is required within an instance document. In the example attribute declaration of Listing 8.14, `use="required"` indicates that this attribute must be explicitly defined every time its element occurs in an XML document using this schema. If you want the attribute to be optional, you could use the following attribute declaration:

```
<xsd:attribute name="empid" type="xsd:integer"
    use="default" value="0"/>
```

Listing 8.15 An optional attribute

The declaration above indicates that the `empid` attribute is not required. If a value for the `empid` attribute is not specified, or if the `empid` attribute doesn't exist at all in an instance document, any validating parser consulting the schema will nonetheless see the attribute as present, with a value "0".

Other valid values for `use` include `optional` (attribute is optional, no default supplied), `fixed` (attribute is optional, value is permanently fixed to the value specified in `value`), and `prohibited` (attribute cannot be included, and does not have a value).

Attribute Declaration Locations
Attribute declarations occur within element declarations. For complex elements, attributes must occur after all child elements have been declared. For example, the following is a legal element and attribute declaration (which adds the `empid` attribute to the `<person>` element):

```
<xsd:element name="person">
  <xsd:complexType>
    <xsd:sequence>
```

```
      <xsd:element name="firstname" type="xsd:string"/>
      <xsd:element name="lastname" type="xsd:string"/>
    </xsd:sequence>
    <xsd:attribute name="empid" type="xsd:integer"
        use="required"/>
  </xsd:complexType>
</xsd:element>
```

Listing 8.16 An attribute within a complex element

Strangely enough, if you want to declare a simple element type (i.e., an element containing only text) with attributes, you need to declare it as a "complex element with simple content" using the special <xsd:simpleContent> element. The declaration looks like this:

```
<xsd:element name="timer">
  <xsd:complexType>
    <xsd:simpleContent>
      <xsd:extension base="xsd:time">
        <xsd:attribute name="accuracy" type="xsd:float"
            use="required"/>
      </xsd:extension>
    </xsd:simpleContent>
  </xsd:complexType>
</xsd:element>
```

Listing 8.17 An attribute within a simple element (declared as a complex element)

According to the schema in Listing 8.17, <timer> elements contain simple content in the form of a time value, and have one required attribute, named accuracy. The <extension> element pertains to data typing and will be explained in the next topic. For now, just accept that the content of this simple element must be a time, and that the content of the accuracy attribute must be a floating point value.

EXAMPLE

This example illustrates an XML schema (Listing 8.18) and XML document (Listing 8.19) describing a school and its staff. The schema says that all of its instances have a root element <school>, which contains one <name>, <address>, and <phone> child element, and unlimited <staff> child elements. The complex and simple element declarations are similar to those you have already seen in this chapter:

```
<?xml version="1.0"?>

<xsd:schema xmlns:xsd="http://www.w3.org/2001/XMLSchema"
    targetNamespace="http://www.school.com"
    xmlns="http://www.school.com"
    elementFormDefault="qualified">
  <xsd:element name="school">
    <xsd:complexType>
      <xsd:sequence>
        <xsd:element name="name" type="xsd:string"/>
        <xsd:element name="address" type="xsd:string"/>
        <xsd:element name="phone" type="xsd:string"/>
        <xsd:element ref="staff" maxOccurs="unbounded"/>
      </xsd:sequence>
      <xsd:attribute name="snumber" type="xsd:integer"
          use="required"/>
    </xsd:complexType>
  </xsd:element>
  <xsd:element name="staff">
    <xsd:complexType>
      <xsd:all>
        <xsd:element name="firstname" type="xsd:string"/>
        <xsd:element name="lastname" type="xsd:string"/>
        <xsd:element name="subject" type="xsd:string"/>
      </xsd:all>
      <xsd:attribute name="id" type="xsd:integer"
          use="required"/>
      <xsd:attribute name="homeroom" type="xsd:integer"
          use="optional"/>
    </xsd:complexType>
  </xsd:element>
</xsd:schema>
```

Listing 8.18 school.xsd

The following Listing (8.19) is a legal XML document, according to the schema in Listing 8.18. Note that we can include the child elements of `<staff>` in any order, because we grouped the elements within an `<xsd:all>` tag in the schema:

```
<?xml version = "1.0" encoding = "UTF-8"?>
<school xmlns="http://www.school.com"
```

```
    xmlns:xsi="http://www.w3.org/2001/XMLSchema-instance"
    xsi:schemaLocation="http://www.school.com school.xsd"
    snumber="001">
  <name>Turner Fenton Secondary School</name>
  <address>5397 Kennedy Road South</address>
  <phone>(555)555-1111</phone>
  <staff id="2" homeroom="304">
    <firstname>Paul</firstname>
    <subject>Computer Science</subject>
    <lastname>Fletcher</lastname>
  </staff>
  <staff id="3">
    <firstname>Eric</firstname>
    <lastname>Zipay</lastname>
    <subject>English</subject>
  </staff>
</school>
```

Listing 8.19 school.xml

We could have further restricted the phone number to the form `(###)###-####` using a *regular expression,* saving ourselves even more manual validation efforts. Although Listing 8.19 does not demonstrate the use of regular expressions, we'll investigate them in the next topic, Data Types.

Special Note—the ref Attribute

You may have noticed something different about the schema in Listing 8.18: at first, there appear to be two root elements. We declare the complex element `<school>` near the top of the document, and then another complex element, `<staff>`, farther down, but at the same level. Both of these element declarations occur directly under the root `<xsd:schema>` element.

So how does this work? If you look at the definition for `<school>`, you will see that one of its simple child elements uses the `ref` attribute, instead of a name attribute.

```
. . .
  <xsd:element name="phone" type="xsd:string"/>
  <xsd:element ref="staff" maxOccurs="unbounded"/>
</xsd:sequence>
. . .
```

The `ref` attribute acts as a kind of forward declaration for elements. If you are familiar with C or C++, you can think of the ref as being similar to a function prototype: the `ref` keyword indicates that the definition of an element can be found somewhere else in the schema. The contents of the "staff" declaration (later in the schema) are automatically included as an element of the current sequence.

Thus, `ref` is simply a means of avoiding XML schemas with dozens of levels of indentation. In this case, we used `ref` because, otherwise, the XML schema would have been awkwardly wide. You can use `ref` to "modularize" your documents and avoid hard-to-read, overly nested XML.

SUMMARY

XML schemas define elements and attributes using the vocabulary contained within the XMLSchema namespace. Elements can be either simple (containing only text) or complex (containing other elements). Attributes can only be simple, as XML attributes cannot contain other attributes (or elements). This topic has discussed how to define and restrict the number of elements and order in which elements and attributes can occur in schema instances. The next topic will cover data types, and how to specify further exactly what your elements and attributes can and cannot contain.

Topic: Data Types

In the last topic, we discussed how elements can be one of two types: simple or complex. In reality, these elements are simple or complex only because they contain simple or complex *data types.* Data types define the content of an element or attribute. An element with a complex data type can contain other elements. An element with a simple data type can contain only text. However, XML schemas allow you to refine these data types so that a data type contains exactly the information you want, in the format you want, and is reusable throughout the document. Data types extend the capabilities of XML schemas far beyond those of DTDs.

For example, suppose you were creating an XML schema intended to act as a template for XML documents containing collections of recorded music. You might begin by creating some simple types to contain artist names, album titles, and numbers of songs. You could restrict these types by specifying that the number of songs must be between one and ninety-nine. You could then create a complex data type, perhaps called `media`, which would contain these three simple types. If you are familiar with a structured programming language, you can think of complex data types as being similar to a structure or a class that has only member variables and no methods. Once you have your complex data type, you can start declaring elements that can appear in schema instances, such as `CD`, `LP`, and `cassette`. Each one of these would be declared as an element of type `media`, and would take on the characteristics of the `media` data type.

CONCEPTS

Anonymous vs. Named Types

There are two different ways in which to define data types: anonymously or by name. All the XML schema examples up to this point have used anonymous data types. Anonymous data types are defined inside elements or attributes and can be used only within those elements and attributes. The following element declaration uses an anonymous complex data type:

```
<xsd:element name="band">
  <xsd:complexType>
    <xsd:sequence>
      <xsd:element name="name" type="xsd:string"/>
      <xsd:element name="style" type="xsd:string"/>
    </xsd:sequence>
  </xsd:complexType>
</xsd:element>
```

Listing 8.20 Declaring and using an anonymous data type

The `<band>` element in Listing 8.20 contains a complex data type. Because this data type has no name, it cannot be used outside of this declaration—there is no way to reference it elsewhere in the XML document.

Alternatively, we could have declared the complex data type as a *named* data type, and then referenced it from the element declaration like this:

```
<xsd:complexType name="band_details">
  <xsd:sequence>
    <xsd:element name="name" type="xsd:string"/>
```

```
    <xsd:element name="style" type="xsd:string"/>
  </xsd:sequence>
</xsd:complexType>

<xsd:element name="band" type="band_details"/>
```

Listing 8.21 Declaring and using a named data type

In this case, we define a complex type with the name `band_details`, and then create an element that uses the `band_details` data type, thereby inserting the content of that complex data type into the element.

Named data types are usually declared globally (i.e., directly underneath the root `<xsd:schema>` element) so that they can be reused, if necessary, throughout the entire schema.

Simple Data Types

Elements with simple data types can contain only character data and not other elements. A typical simple element declaration looks like this:

```
<xsd:element name="ss_number" type="xsd:string"/>
```

We have so far overlooked the type attribute in this chapter. This attribute specifies the data type of an element. In the example above, the `ss_number` element must contain text, and that text must conform to the built-in data type, `xsd:string`.

Built-In Data Types

XML schema provides no less than forty-one built-in data types that you can use when defining simple types. Most of these data types are common in many programming languages, in one form or another. These data types include strings (`xsd:string`), integers (`xsd:integer`), booleans (`xsd:boolean`), floats (`xsd:float`), and so on. The built-in data types also include XML-specific data types, such as `<xsd:uriReference>`, which must be in the form of a URI (e.g., `"http://www.codenotes.com"`).

When defining data types for attributes, you can also use any of the ten DTD data types. For example, you could use the following attribute declaration to declare an attribute as an NMTOKEN:

```
<xsd:attribute name="room_number" type="xsd:NMTOKEN"
    use="required"/>
```

Note that the DTD data types can be used *only* for attribute data types and not for elements. Generally, it is best to avoid DTD types altogether and use XML schema types; we mention the possibility so you will understand the meaning of the syntax should you ever come across it.

The CodeNotes reference card accompanying this book contains a list of the most useful built-in XML schema types. A complete list of all forty-one built-in data types, with examples of each, can be found on the CodeNotes website CN XM000803.

Defining Simple Data Types with Regular Expressions

In many cases, the forty-one built-in data types will not be restrictive enough when it comes to defining the contents of an element or attribute. For example, suppose you were defining XML documents that contain employee information, and you wanted each `<employee>` element to have an attribute `ssnumber` containing the employee's social security number in the form `nnn-nn-nnnn`. You would not be able to use an integer, or any other numerical data type, because none of these types allows hyphens. In fact, the most restrictive built-in data type you could use would be a string.

The string data type is obviously insufficient, as you don't want instances to allow just any string to appear as a social security number. Instead, you need to define your own simple data type that also enforces the hyphenated format of a social security number, using the `<xsd:simpleType>` schema element. The following is an example of how our `ssnumber` data type could be defined:

```
<xsd:simpleType name="ssnumber">
  <xsd:restriction base="xsd:string">
    <xsd:pattern value="\d{3}-\d{2}-\d{4}"/>
  </xsd:restriction>
</xsd:simpleType>
```

Listing 8.22 Defining a simple data type

The `<xsd:simpleType>` element begins the definition of the data type, which, in this case, is a named data type. The `<xsd:restriction>` element creates a "base" for this definition by restricting the content of our type to the rules governing the `xsd:string` built-in data type. In addition to any further rules we impose, elements using the `ssnumber` data type must always be strings. The `<xsd:pattern>` element is a *facet* of the `xsd:string` data type. In this example, the pattern enforces our rule of three digits, a dash, two digits, a dash, and then four digits.

Facets

Every built-in data type has one or more available facets that you can redefine to restrict the contents of your new data type. In the example above, we are restricting the pattern in which this string must be presented. Some other `xsd:string` facets include `xsd:length` (which defines how many characters can occur in the string) and `xsd:enumeration` (which can be used multiple times within a simple type definition to provide a list of explicit values that elements of this type can contain). A complete list of facets for all the built-in types can be found on the CodeNotes website CN XM000804.

In the example in Listing 8.22, we use the `value` attribute of the `<xsd:pattern>` facet to define the pattern in which the social security number is allowed to appear. Patterns in XML schema are specified using *regular expressions.*

Regular expressions are a compact method of representing string patterns, similar to the syntax supported by the Perl programming language. In the SSN pattern above, for example, `\d{n}` will match `n` occurrences of a digit, and the "`-`" character simply matches `-`. So we are matching against three digits, a hyphen, two digits, another hyphen, followed finally by four digits. You can find more information on regular expression syntax on the CodeNotes website CN XM000805.

Since the type we created is a named type, we can then use it elsewhere as the type in an attribute declaration, like this:

```
<xsd:attribute name="ssnumber" type="ssnumber" use="required"/>
```

Note that it is fine for the `type` attribute and the `name` attribute to have the same value, because one refers to an attribute (`name`), and the other to a data type (`type`). Technically, each attribute is said to have its own *symbol space,* which allows this sort of duplicate naming.

Complex Data Types

In the section "Anonymous vs. Named Types" we saw an example of how to define a named, complex data type and then use it elsewhere in the document. Here is another example of a named complex data type:

```
<xsd:complexType name="trade">
  <xsd:sequence>
    <xsd:element name="date" type="xsd:date"/>
    <xsd:element name="time" type="xsd:time"/>
    <xsd:element name="buyprice" type="xsd:decimal"/>
    <xsd:element name="sellprice" type="xsd:decimal"/>
  </xsd:sequence>
</xsd:complexType>
```

Listing 8.23 A named complex data type (trade)

Any element that is of the data type desribed in Listing 8.23 must have child elements `<date>`, `<time>`, `<buyprice>`, and `<sellprice>`. The `trade` data type makes a good *base type,* as any trade will probably have these four characteristics. Suppose, however, that you wanted to create another, more specific data type that included elements applicable only to foreign exchange trades. You could create an `fxtrade` data type and include the `<date>`, `<time>`, `<buyprice>`, and `<sellprice>` element declarations as well as fxtrade-specific declarations, but this would add a lot of repetitive markup to your schema. It is far simpler to simply *derive* the `fxtrade` data type from the existing `trade` data type.

Derivation by Extension

XML schemas allow you to derive new data types from existing data types. There are two ways of deriving a new data type: by *extension,* and by *restriction.* Derivation by extension involves taking an existing data type and appending new elements and attributes to it in order to create a new data type.

For example, we can create an `fxtrade` data type by extending the `trade` data type from Listing 8.23. The `fxtrade` data type could be defined as shown in Listing 8.24:

```
<xsd:complexType name="fxtrade">
  <xsd:complexContent>
    <xsd:extension base="trade">
      <xsd:sequence>
        <xsd:element name="buycurrency" type="xsd:string"/>
        <xsd:element name="sellcurrency"
            type="xsd:string"/>
      </xsd:sequence>
    </xsd:extension>
  </xsd:complexContent>
</xsd:complexType>
```

Listing 8.24 Deriving by extension

The `<xsd:complexContent>` element indicates that this type is going to contain a derivation of an existing class. The `<xsd:extension>` element is used to indicate the base data type from which this new data type is derived. In this case, `base="trade"`, so the `fxtrade` data type uses the `trade` data type as a starting point (or base type). We then add two new element declarations for `buycurrency` and `sellcurrency`, which are specific to the `fxtrade` data type.

Now, any element of data type `fxtrade` must contain *six* child elements: <date>, <time>, <buyprice>, <sellprice>, <buycurrency>, and <sellcurrency>, in that order. Note that when you derive a data type by extension, the new elements you define are *appended* to the end of the list. In other words, you cannot change the element order of the base type; you can only add new elements to the bottom of the list.

Derivation by Restriction

Derivation by restriction allows you to take a base data type and restrict the values of its existing elements and attributes. This is useful if you have a very broad-ranging data type from which you want to derive and then narrow down for a more specific data type.

For example, suppose you wanted to create an afterhourstrade data type. The trade data type from Listing 8.23 would make a good base type, except that you want schema instances to allow afterhourstrades to occur only between 4:30 P.M. and 7:00 P.M. To do this, we can restrict the trade data type as follows:

```
<xsd:complexType name="afterhourstrade">
  <xsd:complexContent>
    <xsd:restriction base="trade">
      <xsd:sequence>
        <xsd:element name="date" type="xsd:date"/>
        <xsd:element name="time">
          <xsd:simpleType>
            <xsd:restriction base="xsd:time">
              <xsd:minInclusive value="16:30:00"/>
              <xsd:maxInclusive value="19:00:00"/>
            </xsd:restriction>
          </xsd:simpleType>
        </xsd:element>
        <xsd:element name="buyprice" type="xsd:decimal"/>
        <xsd:element name="sellprice" type="xsd:decimal"/>
      </xsd:sequence>
    </xsd:restriction>
  </xsd:complexContent>
</xsd:complexType>
```

Listing 8.25 Derivation by restriction

In the example above, we use the element <xsd:restriction> to indicate that we are deriving the contents of this data type by restriction. We then *redefine* the sequence of elements containing <date>, <time>, <buyprice>, and <sellprice>. When deriving by restriction, you must always redefine all of the elements from the base data type, not just the ones you want to restrict. In this case, we want to change only the `time` element.

We limit the hours in which trades are allowed by defining `time` as a simple element type based on `xsd:time`, with the `minInclusive` facet set to "16:30:00" and `maxInclusive` facet set to "19:00:00". This inline type definition restricts the value of `time` to between 4:30 P.M. and 7:00 P.M. Elements of type `afterhourstrade` that have values outside these times will cause a validating parser to report an error.

EXAMPLE

The following example (Listing 8.26) shows a schema that defines the contents of XML documents used to store name and password information for different types of users on a network This schema uses both simple and complex data types and demonstrates derivation through both extension and restriction:

```
<?xml version="1.0"?>
<xsd:schema xmlns:xsd="http://www.w3.org/2001/XMLSchema"
    targetNamespace="http://www.exchange.com"
    xmlns="http://www.exchange.com"
    elementFormDefault="qualified">
  <xsd:element name="system">
    <xsd:complexType>
      <xsd:choice maxOccurs="unbounded">
        <xsd:element name="trader" type="traderuser"/>
        <xsd:element name="administrator"
            type="adminuser"/>
      </xsd:choice>
    </xsd:complexType>
  </xsd:element>
  <xsd:complexType name="user">
    <xsd:sequence>
      <xsd:element name="login" type="login"/>
      <xsd:element name="password" type="xsd:string"/>
    </xsd:sequence>
  </xsd:complexType>
  <xsd:complexType name="adminuser">
    <xsd:complexContent>
      <xsd:extension base="user">
        <xsd:sequence>
```

```
          <xsd:element name="readonly" type="xsd:boolean"/>
        </xsd:sequence>
      </xsd:extension>
    </xsd:complexContent>
  </xsd:complexType>
  <xsd:complexType name="traderuser">
    <xsd:complexContent>
      <xsd:extension base="user">
        <xsd:sequence>
          <xsd:element name="desk">
            <xsd:simpleType>
              <xsd:restriction base="xsd:string">
                <xsd:enumeration value="TO"/>
                <xsd:enumeration value="NY"/>
                <xsd:enumeration value="LN"/>
              </xsd:restriction>
            </xsd:simpleType>
          </xsd:element>
        </xsd:sequence>
      </xsd:extension>
    </xsd:complexContent>
  </xsd:complexType>
  <xsd:simpleType name="login">
    <xsd:restriction base="xsd:string">
      <xsd:length value="8"/>
      <xsd:pattern value="[A-Z]{2}[0-9]+"/>
    </xsd:restriction>
  </xsd:simpleType>
</xsd:schema>
```

Listing 8.26 users.xsd

This schema contains quite a bit of material. Some of the more notable features include:

1. Instance documents must have the root element `<system>`. Within system, an unlimited number of `<trader>` and/or `<administrator>` elements can occur. These two elements both use derived data types.
2. The `user` data type is a base type, containing login and password information that all users of the system must have. The `<login>` element within this type is of a user-defined simple type, `login`, which is defined at the bottom of the example. Lo-

gins must be eight characters long, and are restricted to the form "Letter-Letter-######" (e.g., "CW123456"). Any deviation from this form will produce a validation error.

3. The `adminuser` and `traderuser` complex data types are derived from the `user` base type. Each of these types extends the `user` type by adding elements relevant to the particular kind of user. Administrators have a boolean `<readonly>` element that indicates whether or not they have write access to the system. Traders have a `desk` element, which uses the `xsd:enumeration` facet of `xsd:string` to define its three possible values for the trading desk location: TO, LN, or NY. Any other values will cause a validation error.

SUMMARY

Data types are the backbone of XML schemas. Every element and attribute you declare must have a data type. Data types can either be simple (containing only text) or complex (containing other elements). XML schemas provide forty-one built-in simple data types. You can create your own simple data types by restricting facets of a built-in type. You can create your own named complex types, and derive new data types from them, by restricting existing elements or extending with new ones.

Topic: Practical XML Schema Features

This chapter is by no means an exhaustive reference on XML schemas. The XML schema specification contains numerous other features, some of which are useful, and some of which are simply design aids. The three complete W3C Recommendations for XML schemas can be found at http://www.w3.org/tr. This last topic will cover a few of the more valuable XML schema tools.

CONCEPTS

Mixed Elements

So far in this chapter, we have talked about simple elements (which can contain only character data) and complex elements (which can contain only other elements). With schemas, as with DTDs, it is also possible to define mixed elements, which contain both text and other elements. An example of a mixed element follows:

```
<note>This document is <emp>very</emp> important.</note>
```

The schema fragment to declare a mixed element like the one above looks like this:

```
<xsd:element name="note">
  <xsd:complexType mixed="true">
    <xsd:sequence>
      <xsd:element name="emp" type="xsd:string"
          minOccurs="0" maxOccurs="unbounded"/>
    </xsd:sequence>
  <xsd:complexType>
</xsd:element>
```

Listing 8.27 A mixed element definition

The `mixed` attribute in `<xsd:complexType>` simply indicates that the element can contain text content as well as `<emp>` child elements.

Unique Elements and Attributes

DTDs allow you to specify that an attribute is unique (i.e., its value is not allowed to repeat in the document) by giving it the ID data type. In schemas, you can define elements or attributes as having unique content. With elements, you can make sure the value held between the start- and end-tags is unique, or you can choose an attribute of an element that you wish to have unique, nonrepeating values. Each time an element or attribute that has been declared unique appears in an instance document, it must have a unique value (with respect to the rest of the document). Unique elements and attributes are useful for ensuring that certain pieces of information, such as serial numbers or employee identification numbers, cannot be repeated.

To declare an attribute as unique, you must include an `<xsd:unique>` tag, which uses XPath to find and verify the unique element. The following XML schema fragment declares a unique attribute, `empid`, using the `<xsd:unique>` tag at the end of the fragment:

```
<xsd:element name="company">
  <xsd:complexType>
    <xsd:sequence>
      <xsd:element name="employee" maxOccurs="unbounded">
        <xsd:complexType>
```

```
        <xsd:sequence>
          <xsd:element name="name"/>
          <xsd:element name="position"/>
        </xsd:sequence>
        <xsd:attribute name="empid" type="xsd:integer"
            use="required"/>
      </xsd:complexType>
    </xsd:element>
  </xsd:sequence>
</xsd:complexType>
<xsd:unique name="empid_uniq">
  <xsd:selector xpath="employee"/>
  <xsd:field xpath="@empid"/>
</xsd:unique>
</xsd:element>
```

Listing 8.28 Declaring a unique attribute

The example of Listing 8.28 declares that `empid` is a unique attribute, and thus that all instances of `empid` in instance XML documents must be unique. Although the `<xsd:unique>` tag ensures that the value is unique, it does *not* indicate that `empid` is a required attribute (although the `use="required"` attribute on the actual attribute definition will ensure this is the case). Unique elements are unique only if they are present. If you leave out `use="required"`, then the uniqueness applies only to elements with the attribute.

A few things to note about the `<xsd:unique>` element:

- The `<xsd:selector>` element is used to choose the group of elements for which this element is unique. In this case, it states that the unique attribute will occur within the `<employee>` element. You can include multiple `<xsd:selector>` elements within a single `<xsd:unique>` element.
- The `<xsd:field>` element is used to choose the element or attribute within the selected group of elements. In this case, it is indicating that every instance of `empid` in `<employee>` elements must have a unique value. Attributes being selected must include an @ character before the attribute name. Element selections do not need this character. See Chapter 5 for more details on XPath.
- `<xsd:unique>` elements must always occur within elements (to give them a scope in which to find the selected element group) and must always occur at the end of the element declaration, after all element and attribute declarations.

If an instance of the schema shown in Listing 8.28 were validated against the schema, and had two `<employee>` elements with the same value for `empid`, the validating parser would indicate a validation error.

Keys

Keys create a relationship among data. In XML schemas, you can use keys to create unique elements or attributes that must always occur within their parents. You can then use *key references* elsewhere in the schema to ensure that the value of a particular element matches a key value. If you are familiar with relational database systems, schema keys are similar in concept to foreign key constraints, which you might see enforcing a relationship between two tables. If, for example, you have two tables, customers and orders, you will want to make certain that a `customer_id`, referenced in a row of the orders table, exists uniquely in the customer table. Thus, you can be certain that every order is assigned to a valid customer.

Like the unique constraint, keys are declared at the end of the data type definition, and use XPath to reference the elements involved in the key relationship. For example, suppose your schema defines departments in a company and employees within those departments. Each employee is associated with a department (through a parent-child relationship) and associated with a particular position in the department through a key. The declarations in this schema could look like that shown in Listing 8.29:

```
<xsd:element name="department">
  <xsd:complexType>
    <xsd:sequence>
      <xsd:element name="position" maxOccurs="unbounded">
        <xsd:complexType>
          <xsd:sequence>
            <xsd:element name="pname" type="xsd:string"/>
            <xsd:element name="empid" type="xsd:integer"/>
          </xsd:sequence>
        </xsd:complexType>
      </xsd:element>
      <xsd:element name="employee" maxOccurs="unbounded">
        <xsd:complexType>
          <xsd:sequence>
            <xsd:element name="name" type="xsd:string"/>
            <xsd:element name="empid" type="xsd:integer"/>
            <xsd:element name="address" type=""xsd:integer"/>
            <xsd:element name="phone" type="xsd:integer"/>
```

```
            </xsd:sequence>
          </xsd:complexType>
        </xsd:element>
      </xsd:sequence>
    </xsd:complexType>
    <xsd:key name="empid_key">
      <xsd:selector xpath="position"/>
      <xsd:field xpath="empid"/>
    </xsd:key>
    <xsd:keyref name="empid_ref" refer="empid_key">
      <xsd:selector xpath="employee"/>
      <xsd:field xpath="empid"/>
    </xsd:keyref>
  </xsd:element>
```

Listing 8.29 Using keys and key references

In the example above, the root element can have two children: `<position>` and `<employee>`. The `<position>` element contains position names and the employee numbers that fill the positions. The `<employee>` element also contains employee numbers, as well as names, addresses, and phone numbers.

At the bottom of Listing 8.29, we declare a key and a key reference. The `<xsd:key>` states that every instance of `<position>` must have an `<empid>` element, and that every <empid> must have a unique value not to be repeated by other `<empid>` elements in the document. The `<xsd:keyref>` states that every instance of `<employee>` must contain an `<empid>` element, and that every `<empid>` element value must match up with one that appears in a `<position>` element elsewhere in the document. If an instance contains an `<employee>` element whose `<empid>` element does not match with one in a `<position>` element, a validating parser will give an error.

Some things to remember about keys are:

- `<xsd:key>` must always occur at the end of an element declaration, after all child elements and attributes have been declared.
- Elements or attributes selected by an `<xsd:key>` must always be present in the instance document, must be unique, and cannot have null values.
- Elements or attributes selected by an `<xsd:keyref>` must always have a corresponding element or attribute with the same value.

Using Multiple Schemas

XML schemas can be combined so that you can use the vocabularies defined in more than one schema in your instance documents. You might want to combine schemas if, for example, you had several schemas for different subject matter (say, business addresses and employee data), and you wanted to combine them for use in a single type of instance document (in this case, perhaps a citywide roster of stores with full employee information).

There are three ways in which you can combine multiple schemas:

Combining Schemas in the Same Namespace

You might have two schemas using the same namespace if, for example, you had a general namespace for all of your company information, from stock departments to employees, with a schema for each type of information. If you wanted to create instance documents that could combine two or more of these schemas, you would use the `<xsd:include>` element.

The `<xsd:include>` tag allows you to add existing schemas to a new schema that you are creating by providing the existing schemas' filenames. All schemas you include must be in the same namespace as the schema in which you include them. A typical schema using `<xsd:include>` might look like the following:

```
<xsd:schema xmlns:xsd="http://www.w3.org/2001/XMLSchema"
    targetNamespace="http://www.mycompany.com"
    xmlns="http://www.mycompany.com"
    elementFormDefault="qualified">
  <xsd:include schemaLocation="employees.xsd"/>
  <xsd:include schemaLocation="departments.xsd"/>
</xsd:schema>
```

Listing 8.30 A schema including multiple schemas in the same namespace

In the schema above, the `employees.xsd` and `departments.xsd` schemas are included into the new schema—both of the included schemas must, in their own source, have declared themselves to be in the `http://www.mycompany.com` namespace.

Combining Schemas in Different Namespaces

Obviously, not all schemas you want to combine will be in the same namespace. For example, suppose you have two schemas for technical documentation, one of which is in a namespace for class references, and another of which is in a namespace for user manuals. You want to combine them to produce a namespace for some web pages that put together reference material with some instructional material. Unfortunately, the root schemas are in different namespaces, so you can't simply use <include>.

Fortunately, this problem can be solved with the <xsd:import> element as shown in Listing 8.31:

```
<xsd:schema xmlns:xsd="http://www.w3.org/2001/XMLSchema"
    targetNamespace="http://www.mycompany.com"
    xmlns="http://www.mycompany.com"
    xmlns:um="http://www.usermanuals.org"
    xmlns:cr="http://www.creference.com">
    elementFormDefault="qualified">
  <xsd:import namespace="http://www.usermanuals.org"
      schemaLocation="usermanual.xsd"/>
  <xsd:import namespace="http://www.creference.com"
      schemaLocation="creference.xsd"/>
</xsd:schema>
```

Listing 8.31 Importing existing schemas into a new schema

This schema imports two schemas in different namespaces using the <xsd:import> element. In the <xsd:schema> root element, we associate two prefixes with each of those imported namespaces (um for user manuals and cr for code references). Now, throughout the new schema, we can use data types declared within the usermanuals and creference namespaces. For example, if you had declared a class data type in http://www.creference.org, you could use a line like this in your new schema:

```
<xsd:element name="special_class" type="cr:class"/>
```

The element declaration above declares an element called <special_class>, which uses a data type declared within the creference namespace, namely cr:class.

Using Multiple Schemas in an Instance Document

Instead of creating a new schema that includes or imports other existing schemas, you may simply want to reference more than one schema in an instance document. This is useful if you want to have your instance document use element arrangements defined by two or more schemas, but you don't want to create a schema to enforce this new combined template.

An instance document using two different schemas might look like this:

```
<webdoc
    xmlns:cr="http://www.creference.com"
    xmlns:um="http://www.usermanuals.org"
    xmlns:xsi="http://www.w3.org/2001/XMLSchema-instance"
    xsi:schemaLocation="http://www.creference.com
        creference.xsd
        http://www.usermanuals.org
        usermanuals.xsd">
  <cr:classdefinition>
    <!-- use class reference elements -->
  </cr:classdefintion>
  <um:description>
    <!-- describe class with user manual elements -->
  </um:description>
</webdoc>
```

Listing 8.32 Using multiple schemas in a schema instance

In the above example, we associate two different prefixes (`um` and `cr`) with the two namespaces we want to use. The `xsi:schemaLocation` attribute is then used to indicate two sets of namespaces and schema filenames, instead of just one. Throughout the instance document, we can then use the `um` and `cr` prefixes to access the vocabularies defined by those schemas. A validating parser will validate the document against *both* schemas, reporting an error if either one's rules are broken. However, we have to be careful to always use the correct prefix on every element.

HOW AND WHY

What Can't Schemas Do?

Though schemas present a significant improvement over DTDs for defining rules to govern XML documents, they still can't do everything.

For example, schemas can't allow or disallow certain elements or attributes depending on the value of others. For example, you can't say that a `<person>` element can have a `<retirementbonus>` element only if the `<person>` has an `age` attribute whose value is over sixty-five. XML schemas also do not allow you to compare two element or attribute values to make sure one is greater or lesser than another—for example, you can't say that a `<maximum_size>` element must have a greater value than a `<minimum_size>` element.

Many of these problems can be overcome by using additional technologies such as XSLT and XPath to further transform documents and enforce rules like the ones mentioned in the previous paragraph. Because schemas are XML, they can be extended by XML technologies, which gives them an even greater advantage over alternate-grammar templates like DTDs.

Why Isn't Everyone Using Schemas?

Again, the schema definition is much newer than the DTD definition. Many of the early adopters of XML (such as Java) have a tremendous amount of infrastructure based on the DTD definition. Converting these systems over to schemas will take time and compelling need. For example, you should expect that the J2EE deployment descriptors will be based on DTDs for many years to come.

SUMMARY

Some of the more useful features of XML schemas are the ability to provide keys, reference those keys to make connections between data elements, and import and include schemas from multiple namespaces into other schemas or schema instances. XML schemas also provide a wide range of other less prominent features, some of which are described in a supplement to this chapter on the CodeNotes website CN XM000806. Schemas provide a considerably greater number of features than DTDs offer. By extending schemas with related XML technologies (such as XPath), you can use XML schemas to impose almost any restrictions on XML documents.

Chapter Summary

XML schemas, like DTDs, provide a means of controlling the layout and content of your XML documents. Unlike DTDs, schemas allow restriction of both attribute and element content. Schemas allow the use of forty-one different base data types, the creation and derivation of customized simple and complex data types, and much more control over choice, order, and substitutability of elements and attributes.

XML schemas exist in namespaces, which are used to represent the vocabularies created within the schemas. All XML schemas rely on a vocabulary in a namespace defined by the W3C, which can be used to validate the schema in order to ensure that the schema is correctly designed. An XML schema allows you to control how its instances are arranged, and can be used to ensure consistency across multiple XML documents.

Index